THIRD-PARTY MOVEMENTS
IN THE UNITED STATES

WILLIAM B. HESSELTINE
Professor of History
The University of Wisconsin

AN ANVIL ORIGINAL
under the general editorship of
LOUIS L. SNYDER

D. VAN NOSTRAND COMPANY, INC.
PRINCETON, NEW JERSEY

TORONTO   LONDON

NEW YORK

TO

JOHN DONALD HICKS AND ANNA MAE DAVIS—
THE STUDY AND PRACTICE OF THIRD-PARTY POLITICS. . . .

———————————————————

D. VAN NOSTRAND COMPANY, INC.
120 Alexander St., Princeton, New Jersey (*Principal office*); 24 West 40 St., New York, N.Y.
D. VAN NOSTRAND COMPANY (Canada), LTD.
25 Hollinger Rd., Toronto 16, Canada
D. VAN NOSTRAND COMPANY, LTD.
358, Kensington High Street, London, W.14, England

PREFACE

In many lands, political dissent has often taken a violent, revolutionary turn, and groups defeated at the polling places have resorted to the bayonet to advance their cause. The story of political dissent in the United States is both brief and peaceful. Not even the Communists have overtly asserted an intention to overthrow the government or to make basic alterations in American constitutional forms. There has been, indeed, a native American radicalism, stemming from both a basic artisan tradition and an inherited yeoman tradition, just as there has been a native American conservatism, yet both "radicals" and "conservatives" have normally found political homes in each of the two major parties.

Although the number of separate "parties" in states and cities runs into the hundreds, their careers have been brief, their impact transitory, and their very names lost from memory. Few "third" parties have conducted national campaigns, and only a bare half-dozen can truthfully be said to have influenced national elections. Yet, by voicing grievances and by proposing panaceas, third parties have exerted significant influence upon the policies and programs of major parties. In a curiously anomalous manner, third parties have bolstered the traditional American two-party system.

My thanks are due to the cooperative and helpful staff of the State Historical Society of Wisconsin, and to my colleague David A. Shannon, who has shared with me his special insights into the behavior of Socialists and Communists. My debt to Richard H. Abbott and Rex G. Fisher, research assistants in the University of Wisconsin, for ferreting out vanished third parties, for critical judgment in marshaling material, and for selecting illustrative documents cannot be adequately expressed. I can only regret that I have failed to learn all that they have taught.

Madison, Wisconsin   WILLIAM B. HESSELTINE
September, 1962

3

TABLE OF CONTENTS

Part I

THIRD-PARTY MOVEMENTS IN THE UNITED STATES

— 1 —

THE AMERICAN
TWO-PARTY SYSTEM

The American two-party system has ever been a puzzle to Americans and a mystery to foreign observers. The United States stretches across a continent. Its land includes seacoast and river valleys, mountains and plains, swamps and deserts. Its climates range from the near frigid to the almost tropical. Its people came from various racial stocks and cultures. They live in crowded cities and in sparsely settled rural regions. They are industrial laborers, farmers, merchants, transportation workers, miners, clerks in offices and stores, government employees, and school teachers. Yet in all the diverse land and among a people who all have a right to vote, there have been, traditionally, but two political parties.

Both foreign and domestic critics find fault with the American two-party system. The two parties—so the commentators have said for a century and a half—do not differ fundamentally from one another. Democrats and Republicans, and before them Whigs and Jacksonians, were essentially alike. Bankers and day laborers, farmers and storekeepers were in each political party, and neither party represented a clear-cut division of economic interests or a clearly defined special program or policy. "We are all Republicans, all Federalists," said Thomas Jefferson, as he was inaugurated President of the United States.

Yet, strangely enough, both Jefferson and the critics were touching the essential feature of the American political system. American democracy is, fundamentally, government by unanimous consent. We are all—or practically all—agreed on the forms of government, on its objectives, and on its procedures. The American people, with practical unanimity, are agreed that the party which polls the majority vote shall conduct the government. In other lands and at other times, defeated groups have appealed to arms from the verdict of the ballot box and have sought to overthrow the government by force. In the United States, the defeated party waits for and works toward the next election.

This democratic "government by unanimity" has come about through the willingness of the victorious parties to make concessions and adjustments to the will and wishes of the minority party. The process has been made easier because each of the dominant parties contained within itself diverse groups and discordant elements which are held together by compromise. No major political party in America has ever been single-mindedly committed to a rigid program. Each party has contained liberals and conservatives, reactionaries and radicals. No major party has represented only the interests of a single region. Instead, each party has attempted to appeal to rural and urban voters, Easterners and Westerners. The appeal to diverse groups and regions has resulted in platforms which candidates for office can interpret to suit local groups. Once they come into power, the party leaders strive to harmonize the differing factions and to put into operation a program which satisfies as many groups as possible.

The history of American politics illustrates both the basic unanimity of the American people and the manner in which compromise and conciliation have worked to establish the two-party system. At the close of the American Revolution there was but one "party" in the new United States. They were the "Patriots" who had supported the revolution against Britain. The Tories, who had kept their allegiance to the crown had been either driven from the country or forced out of political affairs. Yet the Patriots were by no means a single, integrated group. Some were wealthy squires like George Washington; some, like Benjamin Franklin, were representatives of an artisan tradition. Others were yeoman farmers, heirs of a tradition of the sturdy yeomanry of England, while still others felt themselves to be especially chosen as trustees to make a new society which would glorify God. Some were wealthy planters; some, merchants; some, laborers; some, poor frontiersmen. Yet, despite all their differences in culture and tradition, in economic interest, and in social condition, they were unanimous in opposition to kings and nobility and in their faith that men in America could solve their own problems. The revolutionary leaders worked hard to bring harmony among the groups and between the different interests. Despite the difficulty of their task, they successfully conducted the Revolutionary War and weathered the turmoil and uncertainties of a half-dozen years of weak government under the Articles of Confederation. The so-called "Critical Period" ended with the adoption of the Constitution and the inauguration of a new government.

The Founding Fathers who gathered in Philadelphia in 1787 to reorder the government of the United States represented diverse and conflicting regional and economic interests. There were, indeed, no laborers or plowmen among them, but some of them had risen from manual labor and farming toil and shared the traditions of yeomen and artisans. Others were squires with a concept of public duty and civic responsibility, and some were heirs of a trustee tradition which compelled them to seek a well-ordered society. They all agreed on the need for a stronger government. They agreed in opposition to a monarchy. Within the framework of their agreement the delegates compromised their differences, adjusted their various schemes and ideas, and emerged from the Convention with a workable instrument of government. It was not, as George Washington explained, exactly what any single delegate or group had wanted. In ratifying conventions within the states, critics severely attacked the Constitution, and forced its supporters to agree to add a Bill of Rights which would protect citizens from aggressive acts by the Federal government.

First Parties. Out of the controversy over the Constitution two groups—not quite "parties"—emerged: Federalists who supported the Constitution, and Anti-Federalists who charged that it was the work of designing men, mostly of the propertied groups—who sought power to protect their economic interests. Yet when the Federalists won, the Anti-Federalists ceased their opposition and gave their support—critical support, it often was—to building the new government. Government by unanimity had received its first experience.

There was no unanimity, however, on the program advanced by some of the victorious Federalists. The Federalists organized the government, George Washington became President, and Congress created courts and government departments. Soon Alexander Hamilton, Secretary of the Treasury, proposed funding the national debt, assuming the Revolutionary War debts of the states, establishing a national bank, and protecting manufactures with a tariff. This was giving force and direction to the new government which some of its supporters had never intended. Opponents in Congress and in the states protested and organized, and soon Thomas Jefferson, Secretary of State, assumed the leadership of the opposition. He formulated the doctrine that the Constitution created a government of limited powers and contended that the document should be strictly construed. In Jefferson's philosophy the common man—yeoman farmers and village artisans, primarily—could be trusted to make wise decisions, and governmental powers should be exercised by the states, which were closer to the people and more responsive to their will than the federal government. In addition, Jefferson organized the opponents of Hamilton's program and arrayed his followers, who called themselves Democratic-Republicans, against the Federalists. Thus was born the American two-party system.

In 1800, Jefferson's party, which was a composite of Southern planters, yeomen farmers, frontiersmen, and city workers, won control of the federal government. As President, Jefferson attempted to undo and to modify some of the acts of the Federalists but, fundamentally, the governmental system remained unchanged. Out of office, the Federalists took up the role of opposition, found strength in the states, and sometimes reverted to a "Jeffersonian" advocacy of States' Rights. For two terms, Jefferson administered the government in a manner indistinguishable in essence from that of the Federalists. He built and strengthened his party, and was able to hand the Presidency over in 1809 to his able cohort, James Madison. Eight years later Madison's Secretary of State, James Monroe, succeeded to the Presidency. After repeated failures for 16 years the Federalist Party disappeared and in 1821 Monroe received all but one of the electoral votes to succeed himself.

The complete dominance of the Democratic-Republican

Party did not last long. One newspaper named Monroe's administration "The Era of Good Feeling," but the good feeling was only on the surface. Intense rivalries between followers of John Quincy Adams, Henry Clay, and Andrew Jackson led to the formation of new parties. In 1825 Adams won the Presidency and Henry Clay joined him, while Jackson and his supporters blocked policies which Adams and Clay formed, and worked to build up a Jackson Party. The Jacksonians called themselves Democrats while the National Republicans, Clay's followers, declaring that Jackson was a tyrant and his men "Tories," eventually borrowed the English name "Whig" to signify their opposition to the "reign of King Andrew." For six presidential elections, from 1832 to 1852 the Whigs survived; twice they won the Presidency (with William Henry Harrison in 1840 and General Zachary Taylor in 1848) and each time their President died in office. By 1856 the Whigs had been so badly defeated and were so divided— someone called them a "party of organized incompatibility"—that they disappeared from politics as a separate organization. Remnants of the Whigs found political homes in the Democratic or in the new Republican Party.

Democrats and Republicans. From 1856 to 1960 the two dominant parties bore the names "Republican" and "Democrat." Winning power in 1860, largely as a result of a split among the Democrats, the Republicans retained the Presidency, and for the most part the Congress, until 1884. In that year the Democrats elected Grover Cleveland, who lost to Republican Benjamin Harrison in 1888, but who was re-elected four years later. The Republicans regained control in 1896, kept it until 1912 when Woodrow Wilson won—largely as a result of a Republican split—and recovered their position in 1920. In 1932, Democratic Franklin Roosevelt won the Presidency. In 1952 the Republicans elected Dwight Eisenhower. In 1960 the Democrats returned to power with the narrow election of John Kennedy. Despite long periods out of office, and serious internal dissensions in each party, neither the Democratic or Republican Parties succumbed as did the Federalists and the Whigs.

Part, indeed, of the reason for the survival of the two rival organizations has been the success of each in harmonizing differences in their ranks. Only twice have they failed. Once was in 1860 when a divided Democracy enabled the Republicans to win power. The other was in 1912 when Theodore Roosevelt divided Republican strength with his Progressive Party and gave success to the Democrats. On all other occasions, serious internal dissensions have been resolved by compromises in programs and platforms, by balancing offices and distributing patronage between the factions. Except for the Progressives in 1912, no third party has threatened to replace one of the major parties.

Role of Third Parties. There were, of course, third parties. Counting city parties, local parties, and parties which had strength only in a single state, the number of third parties in the United States history ran into the hundreds. In the American political vocabulary, any party challenging the two major parties was a "third" party, and no one ever attempted to rank the minor parties in the order of size and importance. Thus the Equal Rights Party, the Loco-Foco Party, the Farmer-Labor Party, the Socialists, Women's Righters, Greenbackers, Vegetarians, Free Soilers, Populists, Communists, Anti-Masons, Prohibitionists, Workers, Constitutional Unionists, Antimonopolyites, Liberals, and Antirenters were all "third" parties. Some had very real significance, others were only vehicles for the expression of minor discontents, still others have been splinter groups in momentary disagreement with major—or even minor—party practices, while a few have been "satellite" parties revolving in the orbit of major parties and working primarily to influence the candidates or the program of the dominant party.

Yet, despite the number of third parties and the often small vote which they polled, the minor groups played a significant role in American political history and made their contribution to the maintenance of the American system of government by unanimity. Often third parties voiced dissents and made sufficient headway at the polls to force the attention of the political managers of the major parties. Often the threat of a third party modified the program of a controlling group. Frequently third parties were the vehicle through which a new idea or policy was launched and tested. When a new proposal met a favorable reception it was adopted by a major party.

In a negative sense, too, third parties served to test new programs, and many of their proposals failed to win support and were discarded. Some third parties could list the number of their proposals which were later enacted into law by other parties. At the same time the pathway of American political history was littered with discarded ideas which were once the darlings of third parties. Such, too, was the record of candidates, politicians, and managers. Some won their spurs in third parties and rose to power in major parties, while unresponsive voters retired other hopeful leaders from the political arena.

Third Parties played a significant part in American political history—even in the maintenance of the traditional "two-party" system. An understanding of their rises and falls contributes depth and meaning to the American democratic system.

— 2 —

ANTIMASONRY AND OTHER PROTESTS

Origins. Even in the beginnings of American political parties, while the Hamiltonian Federalists and the Jeffersonian Democratic-Republicans were organizing, there were occasional local candidates, voicing a discontent with both major groups, who ran for local offices under the auspices of committees or "political associations." Though a few won local office, none achieved election to Congress or to state offices. There was, however, no reason to suppose that all voices and all aspirations could be embodied in the Federalist or Republican ranks.

In early Congresses, individual dissents were rare and usually took the form of a Federalist or a Jeffersonian voting with the other party on a specific issue. But active revolt came in 1806 when Virginia's John Randolph, chairman of the House Ways and Means Committee, broke with Thomas Jefferson. Randolph had warmly supported Jefferson and Madison when they challenged Alexander Hamilton's plans and as they formulated resolutions, passed by Kentucky's and Virginia's Legislatures, denouncing Federalist concentration of national power and asserting that sovereign states had entered a compact to create a federal government of limited power. But, to Randolph's mind, Jefferson as President violated his own principles. He annexed Louisiana without Constitutional sanctions, tried to get an appropriation to annex Florida, and wanted a nonimportation act to check British interference with American commerce. Randolph opposed each, and, finally, when Jefferson proposed buying off the claims of the Yazoo Company which had bribed the Georgia Legislature to get lands, Randolph rebelled. He asserted that he and his supporters were a "third something"—a "tertium quid"—neither Federalist nor Republican, but adherents of the States Rights which Jefferson had abandoned. This was revolt and Jefferson manipulated Randolph out of power. He did not win enough support to form a third party, but he was a prophet of many more far-reaching revolts to come.

Two decades later while party alignments were breaking down, the first real third party made its appearance. John Quincy Adams as President and Henry Clay as Secretary of State led the National Republicans who advocated a program including a protective, federally supported tariff, internal improvements and a national bank. Opposed to the National Republicans, whose support came largely from men of wealth and influence, were Jacksonian Democrats without a practical program but sympathetic to states' rights and opposed to internal improvements. In New York, the Federalists had disappeared and the National Republicans were weak. An "Albany Regency," headed by Jacksonian Martin Van Buren dominated the state. It showed little interest in completing the Erie Canal or constructing connecting branches. The situation bore hard on the area from Rochester west—a "Burned-Over District"—wherein already enthusiastic revivals, humanitarian-reform movements, and utopian-social experiments had sprouted. The area was seeded for political revolt, and this the Antimasonic Party inspired.

Perhaps an undercurrent of hostility to the Masonic order had been mounting for some years. The Freemasons had served as an important agency in the American Revolution and Masons were prominent in drafting the Constitution and instituting the new government. In their ranks were George Washington, Benjamin Franklin, Lafayette, and Patrick Henry. Yet, in time it appeared that Masons held the highest offices in the land, accumulated property, and constituted themselves an aristocratic and oath-bound clique. Critics pointed out that the order was English in origin, created secret titles of nobility, used wine in its rituals, and made sacrilegious use of Christian symbols. In 1821 the Presbyterian Synod of Pittsburgh declared Freemasonry "unfit for professing Christians," and in 1823 the Methodist General Conference prohibited its ministers from joining the order.

The criticisms seemed to have substance as the strange case of William Morgan developed. Morgan was an itinerant stonecutter of Batavia, New York who had written a book *Illustrations of Masonry* which exposed the secrets of the order and set forth the dread and solemn oaths which bound Freemasons to support, employ, and deal with one another. While his book was being printed, Morgan was arrested for theft. Released on this charge, he was promptly jailed for a debt of $2.69. The next day —it was September 12, 1826—someone paid his debt. As Morgan left the jail a band of Masons kidnapped him and hurried him in a carriage to Fort Niagara. Perhaps his kidnappers planned to drive him into Canada. At Fort Niagara their plans changed, and, presumably, they roped and weighted their victim and sank him in the river.

The tale of Morgan's certain abduction and probable murder brought investigations, and it quickly appeared that Masons were obstructing the inquiries. Masonic sheriffs, judges, and jurymen prevented indictments, and furious indignation spread through the Burned-Over District. It now became political. In the spring of 1827 a few town meetings resolved against Masons holding office. Protest meetings denounced the order, Morgan's book appeared, was read and believed, pamphlets repeated the charges against Masonry, voluntary committees began their own investigations. In the summer, Thurlow Weed, editor of the Rochester *Telegraph,* became convinced that Masons were using political power to prevent justice in the Morgan case and to discriminate against the best interests of the region. With his support, Antimasons held nominating conventions in counties in western New York and elected 15 members of the state assembly. Excitement over Morgan's disappearance had contrived with regional dissatisfaction to produce a new party. It had produced one leader, and now others—William Henry Seward, Frederick Whittlesey, Francis Granger—joined. (*See Document No. 1.*)

Development. Early in 1828 Weed began to publish the Antimasonic *Enquirer*. The paper denounced Masonry and the Masonic Regency, and worked both to support the Antimasonic Party and the presidential campaign of John Quincy Adams. The *Enquirer* picked up subscribers in southeastern Pennsylvania—a region filled with Quakers, Mennonites, Amish, and Dutch-Reformed religious bodies—and in western counties where Scotch-Irish Presbyterians were strong. It spread into Vermont. In the summer of 1828, Antimasonic papers began in Lancaster, Pennsylvania and in Boston, Massachusetts. In the elections, Weed failed to get a combination ticket of National Republicans and Antimasons, but the elections gave Andrew Jackson a bare electoral majority in the state while the Antimasons increased their legislative strength to four Senators and seventeen Assemblymen.

In Pennsylvania the Antimasons made a poor run for Congress. In Vermont an Antimason narrowly missed election to Congress and contested the victory of his rival. In Massachusetts, mass meetings endorsed candidates and chose committees to promote the party.

The showing in the elections of 1828 encouraged the promoters of Antimasonry, and attracted ambitious politicians. In Pennsylvania Thaddeus Stevens, master of intrigue and invective, assumed leadership of the party. In 1829, Antimasons organized and ran candidates for Governor and Congress in Pennsylvania, elected Weed to the New York assembly, and won seats in several state legislatures. The next year saw more growth and even Antimasonic stirrings in Ohio and in Rhode Island, while in New York the National Republicans accepted the candidates of the Antimasons for Governor and Lieutenant-Governor and almost carried the state. Early in 1830 Weed began publishing the Albany *Evening Journal* which combined attacks on Freemasonry with a vigorous advocacy of internal improvements.

Despite Weed's efforts, the Antimasons in other states did not espouse an economic program. The Antimasons of Pennsylvania were strongest among groups which opposed the state-built system of canals. On the other hand, Thaddeus Stevens obtained a Pennsylvania charter for the Bank of the United States while Weed showed no enthusiasm for banks. Without a coherent economic program, the Antimasonic Party seemed only a conglomeration of local dissenters. There was, however, another element of cohesion: Antimasonry expressed a deep-seated American fear that secret cabals might conspire to overthrow liberty. Under the pressures of the Anti-masonic movement—rather than a result of laws by political Antimasons in legislatures or in Congress, many Masonic lodges disbanded, many Masons quit the order, and Masons running for office took care to disassociate themselves from conspicuous support by the fraternity. Other societies and college fraternities—notably the Phi Beta Kappa Society—abandoned secrecy.

Political Antimasonry continued to gain in strength. In 1830, Pennsylvanians elected six Antimasons to Congress, and Vermont's Antimasons ran ahead of Democrats and the legislature had to choose the Governor. The next year the Antimasonic candidate became Governor of Vermont. In Massachusetts Ex-President John Quincy Adams, ever ready to suspect secret conspiracies, was elected to Congress in November, 1830. Already Adams had begun to flirt with Antimasonry and to hope the party would help send him back to the White House.

By the fall of 1831 the leading spirits of Antimasonry had determined to unite the state groups into a national party and run a candidate for President in 1832. Some leaders preferred Henry Clay who was a Mason and refused to renounce his membership to obtain the endorsement. They made only polite gestures toward Adams and briefly considered John Marshall and John C. Calhoun. The most likely candidate appeared to be Supreme Court Justice John McLean. But as the Antimasons assembled in convention, McLean sent a note that he intended to support his friend, Henry Clay.

On September 26, 1831, the Antimasonic party assembled in Baltimore. It was the first national nominating convention in America. State and local conventions had earlier offered nominees, though national officers had been nominated by party caucuses in Congress or in state legislatures. The Antimasons proclaimed that theirs was a most democratic system of nomination. In December, the National Republicans, and in May, 1832, the Jacksonian Democrats, following the Antimasonic lead, assembled in convention in Baltimore. The Antimasons, finding that no leading political figure would accept their nomination, finally chose William Wirt of Maryland—once an Attorney-General of the United States. Wirt's nomination was an anomaly. He was a Mason who had not repudiated his membership. He was not a strong candidate, and in the Presidential election popular attention fixed on Henry Clay and Andrew Jackson, the nominees of the major parties. Wirt polled less than 40,000 popular votes, but he got Vermont's seven electoral votes.

Aftermath. It was an unimpressive showing, and the Antimasonic Party disappeared as a factor in national politics. (*See Document No. 2.*) For most of a decade, however, it continued to influence state politics. Antimasonic support frequently determined close elections and candidates of the Whig Party were generally careful not to identify themselves too closely with Freemasonry. In other ways the party had played a significant role. Perhaps its most outstanding claim to fame was the precedent it set of the national nominating convention—though by 1831 both Democrats and National Republicans were prepared to hold conventions. More important, in the long run, were other effects of Antimasonry. It had alerted the American people to the dangers inherent in secret combinations; it had encouraged dissenters from the ruling cliques to take political action and had cautioned politicians against running roughshod over minority groups and regions, and it had given new popular leaders—Weed, and Seward, and Stevens among the more important—opportunities to test their political wings. Under the leadership of such new men, the Antimasonic elements furnished a popular base for the Whig Party—which was, in fact, a merging of the National Republican and Antimasonic parties.

Workingmen's Party. The Antimasonic Party was essentially a local movement, expressing the dissatisfaction of the "infested district" of New York and the neglected areas of Pennsylvania and Vermont. At the same time urban workingmen in Philadelphia and New York, suffering from changes in technology, the rising factory system, reduction of wages, the growing disparity between rich and poor, began independent political action. Laboring classes felt that the laws bore upon them unequally—especially those providing imprisonment for minor debt and compelling militia service. Without free schools the workingmen faced a future of toil, poverty, and ignorance. In 1827, carpenters in Philadelphia went on strike for a ten-hour day. Other workers came to their aid, and late in the year the Mechanics Union of Trade Associations was formed.

The Mechanics Union launched a political campaign for the fall elections of 1828, demanding public schools and mechanics, lien laws, and denouncing imprisonment for debt, the militia, chartered monopolies, lotteries, the liquor industry, and banks. In the elections most candidates of the Working Men's Party were defeated, but a score who had received endorsement from the Democrats won office. The next year saw a repetition of the experience, and workingmen in other Pennsylvania cities began to organize. By 1830 it seemed that the Working Men's Party would establish a statewide organization. But their success invited attacks from the outside and dissension inside and by 1831 the movement collapsed.

More success met the workingmen of New York. Here a group of reformist "intellectuals" arose to lead the workers and soon there was severe ideological dissension among them. One leader was Thomas Skidmore who advocated a primitive society of agrarian communism, and proposed to reform society by redistributing land. He won some support in 1829 and even had some followers in 1832. Other mechanics followed Frances Wright, Robert Dale Owen, and George Henry Evans in a State Guardianship Party who offered education as the panacea for working-class ills. Momentarily united, the workingmen made a fair showing in city elections in 1829 and elected one state assemblyman. Encouraged by this meager success, and by workers' groups appearing in other towns,

the leaders planned to launch a statewide party. Before
a state convention could be held, factions developed and
an Anti-State Guardianship group challenged the Owen-
ites. (*See Document No. 3.*) In August, 1830, when the
convention endorsed the Democrats the factions divided
and each nominated slates of candidates. With these sets
of office-seekers, each claiming to be the true representatives of the workers, the mechanics were confused and
demoralized. Most of them voted the Jackson ticket. (*See
Document No. 4.*)

In other states there were rudimentary workingmen's
parties which met similar fates. Despite their failures,
they had some significance. They voiced the unhappiness
of laboring men until politicians of orthodox parties
promised to remedy their grievances. Many of the reforms
they advocated were adopted: imprisonment for debt and
compulsory militia service were abandoned, mechanics'
lien laws were adopted, and the movement for free public
education received a fresh impetus. For the most part it
was the Democrats who sponsored the reforms—thereby
adding the support of urban mechanics to counterbalance
the rural accessions which Antimasonry made to the
Whigs.

Antirent Party in New York. Before the decade
passed still another dissenting political movement began
in New York. Stephen Van Rensselaer, heir of a vast
patroonship, died in January, 1839. He was a man of
high character, esteemed by his tenants, partly because
he had failed to collect his rents. His heirs' determination
to collect back rents brought about the first outbreaks of
the Antirent war in New York, that was to last in various
forms through 1845. Direct action—preventing sheriffs
from distraining goods, keeping landlords from collecting
rents—obstructed the fulfillment of legal obligations. In
1840 Antirent associations sprang up in leasehold counties. Organizers made efforts to agitate the tenant cause,
and gain members for the associations. The associations
formed the basis for later political action.

Antirentism became part of a general reform movement seeking to improve man and society. It entered the
lists along with other "isms" to combat the evils of tenancy, Masonry, and rum, and became a channel through
which reformers tried to effect constitutional changes in

the state, and land reforms in the nation. Also it became a medium through which much of the agricultural discontent in New York found expression. Farmers living on worn-out fields and isolated farms found the landlord a convenient scapegoat for their poverty and uncertainty. The movement drew the politicians who saw possibilities in the agitation, and professional reformers as well were attracted to the cause.

In 1840, tenants petitioned the legislature, and their petitions, plus Governor Seward's use of the militia to put down the "Helderberg War"—centering around the Renssalaer tenants—aroused Democrats and Whigs, who began to line up on the issue. Both parties wanted to take credit for investigating Antirent protests, and blamed each other for the uprising.

In 1844 at least two things happened to encourage political action; the tenants killed a sheriff, and public repudiation of force led many of the tenants to turn toward political organization; and in the same year an Assembly judiciary committee turned in a report favoring the landlords. This report convinced tenants it was time to start influencing the choice of electors rather than trying to petition the legislature. On January 15, 1845, the first Antirent state convention met, with 11 counties sending 150 delegates. (*See Document No. 5.*) Such conventions were held yearly until 1851. Once the Antirenters demonstrated their political power, politicians began to intrigue to secure endorsements, and political considerations began to outweigh the original purpose of the Antirenters.

The Antirenters pursued a wise course. In counties where they did not have a plurality of votes, they selected a candidate nominated by one of the two major parties. They held the balance of power in several important counties, and forced both parties to bid for their support. During 1844-48 the Antirenters found the Whigs more responsive than Democrats to ideas of coalition. Outstanding Whigs like John Young, Horace Greeley, and Ira Harris were conspicuous in their support of Antirentism, while Silas Wright, Democratic governor from 1844-46, was uncompromising. In general, the Antirent associations called for legislative action to force landlords to make concessions to tenants.

The tenant farmer was interested in local and specific benefits, not in national or theoretical reforms. Thus, they got into conflict with the National Reform organization out of New York City. The National Reformers, believing land monopoly was the great obstacle to human progress, alarmed conservatives by telling tenants to "Vote Yourself a Farm." George Henry Evans and his supporters were quite ready to use Antirent associations to advance their theories of land reform. At first the Antirenters welcomed the support; professional agitators like Thomas Ainge Devyr (from the New England Workingman's Association) and Alvan Bovay gave valuable assistance. But the farmers began to grow wary of city theorists who were only willing to let them have 160 acres of land apiece. The National Reformers made several attempts to seize control of the Antirent convention, but were beaten back. Ira Harris, Whig politician, who saw these alarming reform doctrines would scare away Whig votes, helped get rid of the Evans men. Thus in 1846 the National Reformers organized their own party and nominated their own state ticket.

In 1845 the Antirenters captured numerous local offices and elected a State Senator. In 1846, the Antirenters supported the Whig nominee for Governor, John Young, against Democrat Silas Wright, who had earned their hatred by forcibly quelling tenant disorders and imprisoning some of their leaders. Results of the election showed Antirenters held the balance of power in the state. Young was elected by 11,572 over Wright. (*See Document No. 6.*) In 1847 the Antirent state convention endorsed 12 men, for various state offices—eight of them were Whig. In 1851, the Antirenters made their last attempt to influence state elections; they endorsed the entire Democratic ticket, causing Whig members to bolt the convention and set up a rival slate. This split virtually ended Antirent political importance.

Antirent agitation had some concrete results. The legislature abolished distress for rent in all new leases, restricted length of leases to not more than five to ten years, and taxed all income derived from rent. This quelled most of the problem of tenures, and left the question one of minor significance. Also, the landlords were finding that tenancy was not the best way to realize income from land while Western-crop competition lowered prices. Anti-rentism died away, leaving only the memory of still another political expression of dissent that could inspire the future.

— 3 —

NATIVISTS AND KNOW-NOTHINGS

Early Nativism. Antimasonry, both as a social movement and a political organization, represented a deep-seated popular suspicion of secret cliques controlling office-holders. Equally as subversive of the democratic system was the bloc vote which committed groups of voters to exercise the suffrage as directed by hidden powers. If votes could be counted in advance, if they were cast in behalf of or at the behest of special economic, religious, or social groups, then the democratic system, which rested on the free decisions of free men, would be perverted. The fear of the bloc vote lay at the base of the Nativist movement. Paradoxically, the Nativists attempted to oppose one alleged interest bloc with another, to organize secret societies, and to proscribe groups of citizens. Their efforts eventually produced the ill-organized and incoherent Know-Nothing Party.

As immigration to the United States grew in the first decades of the nineteenth century, a number of older inhabitants took alarm. The new arrivals seemed to assimilate slowly, and clung tenaciously to their old ways. The Germans kept their language, and the Irish clung to the Catholic church. Both, moreover, depressed the labor market while the Irish, especially, showed considerable political zeal—and usually voted the Democratic ticket. In 1827, in New York City, a local third party, doubtless encouraged by Federalist politicians, offered an "American Ticket." By the middle 1830's, Protestant alarm over the growth of the Catholic church produced fresh anti-Catholic outbursts. In 1834, in the New York *Observer,*

S. F. B. Morse published a series of letters describing the growing menace of popery, alleging that the church was seeking temporal power in America, and asserting that Irish parishioners voted as their priests dictated. Perhaps, indeed, doctrinal disintegration of Calvinism, together with the declining political influence of New England-type Congregationalism, gave impetus to an anti-Catholic crusade. In 1834 a mob burned an Ursuline convent near Boston. Two years later the obscene revelations of Maria Monk, an "escaped nun," sold more copies than any other American book. In 1835, Nativists in New York attempted to organize a state political party. The Native American Democratic Association, basically an expression of antagonism to the clannishness of Irishmen, proclaimed itself a local organization that voters could endorse without putting aside their regular party affiliations. The Nativists opposed Catholics, sought to exclude all foreigners from office, and opposed the immigration of paupers and criminals. In the fall elections the Whigs put up no separate ticket, and the party got 40 per cent of the vote. In the following spring the Native Americans ran Morse for Mayor, but since he was a Van Buren Democrat the Whigs ran a candidate against him—thus killing his chances and injuring the new party. Two years later the Nativists fused with the Whigs and disappeared as a separate party.

In the 1840's a new spate of Nativist activities appeared in New York, Philadelphia, Baltimore, and New Orleans and spread to other metropolitan areas. In general, they were associated with Whigs in local elections and were never able to effect statewide organization. Their principal lines of attack alleged that immigration was a source of pauperism, that immigrants lowered the moral tone of society, took jobs from American working men, and corrupted society by casting ignorant or purchased votes—for the Democrats. The Nativist parties usually proposed requiring 21 years residence before naturalization, preventing election frauds based on immigrant voters, keeping foreigners out of office, and in some cases, keeping the Bible in public schools. In New Orleans, when Democrats illegally naturalized immigrants so they could vote, the reaction enabled the Native American Association to carry the municipal elections of 1841. By

1843 the Whigs had taken over the Nativist, reform program. In St. Louis and Baltimore, in the early 1840's, the Nativists were reformers, and in Baltimore their program had an especial appeal for mechanics.

In New York and Philadelphia, prolonged Democratic control stimulated third parties. In 1845 the Native Americans elected two Congressmen, but riots at the polls served to discredit the movement and efforts to form a state party failed. In New York, the Nativist movement was more openly anti-Catholic than in other cities. There a dispute over use of the Bible in schools and Catholic demands for a share of public funds for parochial schools stimulated Nativist sentiment, while disgust with Democratic favoritism to Irishmen gave it a reformist tinge. In 1844 a Native American ticket promised lighter taxes and better government and won the mayoralty. The next year, however, the group dissolved—partly because Whigs withdrew their support. In 1845 delegates from 14 states assembled in Philadelphia to attempt to form a national "American Party," but their efforts met no success. (*See Document No. 7.*) In 1848 they endorsed Zachary Taylor, the Whig Presidential nominee. Four years later a remnant nominated Daniel Webster, who ignored their support.

Secret Societies. As the political efforts proved unsuccessful, Nativists found expression in secret societies. Although Antimasonry had given lodges and fraternities a momentary setback the Masons quickly revived, and grew both in numbers and in imitators. Among the latter, by the early 1850's were a number of Nativist societies: the Order of United Mechanics, the Order of the Sons of America, the United Daughters of America, the Order of United Americans, and the Order of the Star Spangled Banner. The societies carried on an anti-immigrant and anti-Catholic agitation. In the early 1850's they won substantial support from Protestant churchmen. The American Tract Society published numerous tracts against Catholics and the American Bible Society distributed "Protestant" Bibles. Lyman Beecher, prominent preacher, wrote and preached against the papacy and new revelations from "escaped nuns" appeared. In 1853 the arrival of a papal nuncio to settle a dispute between laymen and clergy in Buffalo touched off a series of riots. An agitator, the "Angel Gabriel," preached in the streets. Soon the propaganda of the secret societies was supplemented by the riotous action of lower-class gangs with a variety of names—Wide Awakes, Black Snakes, Red Necks, Gladiators, Rip Rips, Plug Uglies. They gave battle to Democratic Butt Enders, Double Pumps, and Dead Rabbits.

American Parties. Out of the secret societies and their rowdy allies came a new political movement directed against corrupt political machines thriving on foreign votes, intemperance, illiteracy, pauperism, and crime. A tremendous influx of Irish Catholic immigrants gave new impetus to action, while the chaotic conditions of national parties gave opportunity. The Whig Party was disintegrating and the Democratic Party housed warring elements. In the states, Nativists re-entered politics, succeeded in getting statewide organizations, and in 1856 became a national party, calling themselves the "American Party."

Horace Greeley of the New York *Tribune,* who contended the party had no more substantial unifying principle than an anti-potato-rot party would have, dubbed it the "Know-Nothing Party." It was said that the members of the secret societies—and especially the politically conscious Order of the Star Spangled Banner—answered questions about their activities with "I know nothing about it." The Nativists, indeed, gave Greeley reasons for his observation: the Know-Nothings differed in each state and section of the country. In the Western states, the Know-Nothings were less influenced by anti-Catholic propaganda than by the fear of an immigrant vote. Germans and Scandinavians, rather than Irish, settled the region. In general, the Know-Nothings cooperated with the declining Whigs or the rising Republicans in nominating fusion tickets and eventually they succumbed as separate organizations. In California, Know-Nothings became a reform party with little opposition to either foreigners or Catholics. The reform element, however, lost control as professional politicians captured the leadership and led the party into the Republican fold.

In the Southern states, where neither immigration nor the influence of the Catholic Church constituted immediate local problems, the Know-Nothings played a different role. Essentially they were successors of the Whigs and their unifying theme was opposition to the Democratic Party. In Texas, where there was a Mexican population and a vague memory of having lived, prior to 1835, under a state church, there was a little anti-foreignism, but, for the most part, Texas Know-Nothings gave their attention to issues relating to a state railroad and to the state debt. Florida had few Catholics and welcomed foreign additions to the state's scant labor force. In Louisiana, Catholics joined the party, and in 1855 the Know-Nothings elected a Catholic as governor. In Alabama and Mississippi the Know-Nothings ignored Nativist agitation to concentrate on local issues.

In the border states of the upper South, the Know-Nothings had greater importance. The party was strong in Missouri, Tennessee, Kentucky, and Maryland. In St. Louis, the Germans aligned with the Know-Nothings in opposition to Irish Democrats. In Baltimore, where Henry Winter Davis was one of the prominent leaders, the Know-Nothings had the support of Plug-Ugly hoodlums who wore shoemaker's awls strapped to their knees and terrorized the polling places. In these states, where fear of sectional conflict was great, the Know-Nothings were the party of union and were primarily concerned with the danger involved in the success of a sectional party. Here they were nationalists rather than Nativists. They saw that immigration strengthened Northern states, increased their power in the national government, and threatened Southern institutions and influence. (*See Document No. 8.*) Out of the Southern states came a number of Know-Nothing Congressmen.

The real strength of the Know-Nothings lay in the Northeast. Here the Irish and Catholic immigration, growing spectacularly in the 1840's and 1850's, was greatest. (*See Document No. 9.*) In 1853 an Irish bloc defeated a reform constitution in Massachusetts and all the forces of discontent gathered in the Know-Nothing Party. Anti-slavery people denounced Irish support of the Pierce administration and Catholic refusal to help rescue fugitive slaves. Reformers denounced corruption. In Connecticut, temperance advocates joined the party. In New York, Pennsylvania, and New England the Know-Nothings won rapid support.

The strength of the Know-Nothing movement was revealed in state elections in 1854 and 1855. In 1854 the party sent forty members to the New York legislature, won the Governorship, and had all but two members of the Massachusetts legislature. Pennsylvania and Delaware Know-Nothings combined with Whigs to carry their states. Nine of Indiana's eleven Congressmen that year belonged to the "American Party." The next year "American" governors won in Rhode Island, New Hampshire, Connecticut, Massachusetts, California, and Kentucky, with state tickets carrying the day in Texas, New York, and Maryland. Eight states had Know-Nothing legislatures. In the 34th Congress there were five "Americans" in the Senate and forty-three in the House.

The Know-Nothing success brought few tangible results. The Massachusetts Legislature appointed a "Nunnery Committee"—though there were no nunneries in the state—which toured the state finding no scandals except the scandalous conduct of some of its own members. Connecticut enacted a literacy test for voters and required church property to be held by corporate bodies. In Congress the "Americans" did little. A bill excluding foreign paupers and convicts died in committee, and other proposals for immigration reform never reached committees.

National Americans. The failure to enact any significant national legislation was a symbol of the general weakness and incoherence of the party. Even as it won victories, the party abandoned secrecy with its lodges, rituals, and passwords. In some states the anti-Catholic test was abandoned, and Protestant foreigners were admitted. On other issues before the country there was no unity. The "South Americans" favored territorial expansion and low tariffs; North Americans favored internal improvements, a homestead law, and a protective tariff. The Northerners were infected with antislavery, the Southerners were unionists hoping to still disruptive agitation of the slavery issue. In 1854 the National Council, to reassure Southerners, introduced a new oath pledging members to oppose any attempt to destroy, weaken, or subvert the Union. The Massachusetts Grand Council refused to ratify the innovation. In 1855 when the National Council met in Philadelphia, it accepted, after long debate, a resolution condemning antislavery agitation and declaring Congress had no power to legislate on slavery.

Massachusetts' delegates, led by Senator Henry Wilson, held another meeting to insist on Nativism and anti-slavery. Long before the Know-Nothings held a national nominating convention in 1856 the party was split between its Southern and Northern members.

On February 18, 1856, the National Council met in Philadelphia, debated issues dividing Northern and Southern "Americans" and, four days later, resolved itself into a national convention. When Northern delegates failed to get a commitment to a candidate opposing slavery extension, they withdrew. The remainder nominated Millard Fillmore, Whig Vice President who had succeeded to the Presidency upon the death of Zachary Taylor. Fillmore was no Know-Nothing and had never declared himself in favor of Nativist principles. Angry Northerners held a second convention five days before the new Republican Party met, in hopes the Republicans would combine with them. In the election of 1856, Fillmore carried Maryland and showed some strength in the border states.

The campaign marked the end of the "Americans" as a national party, and it rapidly disappeared in the states. The secrecy and the intolerance of the Nativist parties had made them vulnerable to attack. "Southern Americans" held on for a few years—mostly adopting the accurate but unappealing name of "Opposition Party." Northern Know-Nothings merged into the new Republican Party and furnished it some of its leaders and many of its followers. Yet for all its failures, the Know-Nothing Party gave expression to nationalist sentiments, and perhaps it quickened the Americanization and conformity of foreign groups. Essentially a unionist party, it was unable to withstand the rising tide of sectionalism and to offer a coherent program which could gather support in both North and South.

— 4 —

LIBERTY AND FREE SOIL PARTIES

Slavery's Opponents. Throughout the years that Nativist parties were placing a new, albeit narrow stress on American unity, another group of parties was carrying on an economic and moral crusade against the South and against slavery. Between 1840 and 1852 the Liberty and Free Soil Parties agitated the slavery issue, promoted the idea that the South and the slaveholders constituted a barrier to economic development, and prepared the way for the rise of the Republican Party.

Opposition to slavery was as old as the institution itself. Throughout the colonial period, Quakers and other religious groups expressed hostility to slavery, and many of the leaders of the American Revolution—George Washington, Benjamin Franklin, and Thomas Jefferson among them—declared their opposition on humanitarian and economic grounds, and even because holding men in bondage was out of accord with Revolutionary principles. In the late 1820's, conflicts between tidewater planters and non-slaveholding small farmers of western Virginia brought debates in the Virginia legislature and in a state constitutional convention. Slavery had, indeed, always had political implications. In the Federal Convention it had occasioned controversy among the Founding Fathers, and produced the "three-fifths compromise" by which five slaves were counted as three free men in apportioning representation in Congress. Three decades later, when Missouri applied for statehood, opposition flared against the admission of another slave state—to be settled by a compromise which, in one of its parts, restricted new slave states to the territories admitted south of Missouri's southern border. The controversy came, as Jefferson said, like "an alarm in the night," and, thereafter, there were always some Northern politicians ready to raise the slavery issue, while there was wary tension among Southerners.

Organized opposition to slavery came early in the 1830's when William Lloyd Garrison established the *Liberator* to demand immediate abolition, and founded the New England Antislavery Society. Soon other abolitionists formed the American Antislavery Society, sent agents to organize local societies, and began the publication of newspapers and pamphlets. At first the Antislavery societies appealed to the consciences of men, and scorned political activity. Garrison denounced the Constitution as a slaveholder's document, and called the Union a "League with Hell." He opposed all "human government," and never endorsed political action.

The organizers and officers of the abolition societies made strong appeals to men who shared the trustee tradition in America. As Stewards of the Lord, and especially blessed with an understanding of God's will, men of the trustee tradition believed they should eradicate evils from society. Looming large in their background was the memory of the Puritan commonwealths with their use of the power of the State to enforce moral conduct. Such men might have little patience with Garrison's mystic anarchism, and the more practical among them realized that moral appeals failed to arouse widespread interest. They turned readily to explore the possibilities of political action.

They began by sending petitions to Congress to abolish slavery in the District of Columbia and other federal property. When the Southern-controlled House of Representatives, annoyed by the flood of petitions, passed a "gag rule" to lay all such papers on the table, John Quincy Adams, now a Congressman, took up the cudgels in defense of the petitioners. Already piqued by Southerners who had made his Presidency miserable, and ever ready to suspect furtive conspiracies, Adams imagined that the "Slaveocracy" was secretly leagued to control the government for Southern ends. Soon he was joined by Joshua Giddings who lost no opportunity to expound the evils and dangers of slavery. Encouraged by their acts, abolition societies began questioning candidates of both parties—and presumably cast their votes for office-seekers with antislavery sentiments. This kind of activity, however, contributed to a growing breach in the antislavery organization. The Garrison wing refused to countenance any political activity, while a faction led by Louis and Arthur Tappan, New York merchants, advocated forming a third party on antislavery principles.

Liberty Party. Prominent among the exponents of a third party were Myron Holley and Gerrit Smith of New York, James G. Birney of Michigan who had once been a slaveholder in Kentucky, E. M. Stanton and Joshua Leavitt of Massachusetts, editor of the *Emancipator*, organ of the American and Foreign Antislavery Society. Leavitt called attention to the political power of the South, commented that the Antislavery Society wielded only moral power, and then demanded an antislavery party to meet the Slave Power on its own ground. Concerning the goals of such a party, Leavitt admitted it was impossible to attack slavery in the states (this would always remain a tenet of the Liberty Party) but insisted the party should try to disengage the laws, institutions, and politics from subjection to the slavery influence, and free domestic and foreign policy from its control. (*See Document No. 10.*)

In July, 1839, the national convention of the American Antislavery Society discussed the advisability of separate political parties, but took no formal vote. In October, the Society met in Cleveland, where members voted down two resolutions introduced by Myron Holley pointing toward a separate abolition party. In November, 1839, advocates of political action held their own convention at Warsaw, New York, where they nominated Birney and Francis Lemoyne of Pennsylvania. Birney declined, preferring nomination by the regular body of abolitionists. Lemoyne also refused the dubious honor. Gerrit Smith and Holley then sent out a call for a national Abolitionist nominating convention to meet April 1, 1840, at Albany. One hundred twenty-one delegates from New York and New England attended the convention which proceeded to choose Birney and Thomas Earle of Ohio as standard bearers. This time Birney accepted. Possibly on the suggestion of Smith, delegates gave the new organization the name Liberty Party.

The party made its appearance as a party of protest. It set up no particular campaign organization; its Presidential candidate, Birney, was in England from May until late November. It was slow work to convert antislavery societies into political organizations; Birney had more opposition from antislavery friends than from rival parties. He faced non-human government Garrisonians, and especially Whig abolitionists who were slow to throw away their votes. An insufficient number of Liberty ballots were prepared for the 1840 election, and in some places there were no Liberty ballots at all. The election returns gave Birney a vote of 7,059 (out of an estimated potential of 70,000 eligible voters who were members of abolitionist societies). Even in Massachusetts and Ohio, Birney got less than one per cent of the vote.

After this somewhat abortive attempt in 1840, Liberty Party leaders began a more active attempt to gather support for political antislavery. Abolitionists changed their emphasis from moral to political and economic arguments. Led by men like William Goodell and Joshua Leavitt, antislavery papers and orators began to claim that the slave South placed burdens on the national economy. New England speakers alleged that Southern cotton, not Northern manufacturers, benefited from American commercial negotiations, while newspapers and orators in the Northwest told farmers that an overemphasis on slave-grown cotton and tobacco kept wheat out of the world market. Leavitt and others blamed the Panic of 1837 on the South, and they stated that until the nation was free of the political dominance of the slaveholder, it would never shake his economic dominance. Some pointed to the great market that would be created when the slaves were finally freed. (*See Document No. 11.*) Leavitt in particular was aware of the importance of uniting the growing Northwest in the battle against slavery. He developed a "corn-law argument," which demanded that the federal government cease seeking advantages for the cotton trade and work for repeal of the English corn laws.

The party's platform remained little changed throughout its existence. Besides the general goal of freeing the national government from the grip of the slave power, Liberty men aimed at abolishing slavery in the District of Columbia, in the Territory of Florida, and in any new territories added to the United States. They opposed the three-fifths clause of the Constitution, and the fugitive slave laws. The party, admitting the national government had no control over slavery in the states, promised action on the state level wherever it could organize and succeed in elections. The party pledged itself to foster the commercial interests of the free states, and break the Southern control over the national economy.

This platform caused much dispute in party ranks. A radical element in the party insisted the Constitution was an antislavery document, and the party should campaign against slavery in the states. Lysander Spooner and William Goodell formulated and advocated the argument, but they found little support west of New York. All, however, did agree Congress had no right to establish slavery in the territories. But the greater struggle came over attempts to include new issues in the platform. The party refused to deal with questions of bank, tariff, and internal improvements. Some resolutions of state organizations began to promise that though the party's first effort had to be directed against slaveholding, it would also carry out the principles of "Equal Rights" in all other applicable areas, and support every measure conducive to individual and social freedom. James G. Birney, party standard-bearer in 1840 and 1844, soon found that it was impossible to be a candidate without expressing himself on all issues of current interest. He recognized that the Liberty Party would have to broaden its platform, and wrote Lewis Tappan that "A party that does not take the *whole* of it —but seeks a particular object—will soon . . . become a lost party." Michigan took the lead in advocating departure from the one-idea policy. In February, 1845, Birney and Thomas Foster submitted a platform to the state convention which dealt with powers of the President, Army and Navy, tariff, popular election of more federal officers, corporation policy, and district systems of election. Most of the delegates found these ideas too radical. Bailey, Smith, Leavitt, and Alvan Stewart opposed incorporating any new ideas into the platform; Beriah Green was one of the few Eastern leaders favoring such a move.

The refusal of the main body of the Liberty Party to depart from its one-ideaism induced a minority, centered largely in western New York, to affirm its principles and nominate its own candidates. The faction drafted a platform denouncing monopoly, approving disbanding the Army and Navy, favoring free trade, opposing secret societies, and proposing direct per-capita taxation, including slaves, as a means of forcing emancipation. The group also favored distribution of public lands in small parcels. Adopting the name Liberty League, these insurgents nominated Gerrit Smith for President. Smith, hitherto an opponent of any additions to the abolitionist platform, accepted the nomination. In 1848, in an attempt to get wider support, Smith called a convention of abolitionists in Buffalo; this rump convention, calling itself the National Liberty Party, also chose Smith as its Presidential nominee. Finally, George Henry Evans' organization, the Industrial Congress, meeting in Philadelphia, selected Smith as its choice for the nation's highest office. Smith's slogan, "Free Men, Free Soil, and Free Trade," gave him a plurality of votes in Madison County, New York, and 2,545 votes in New York State.

Editors of the two most influential Liberty papers, Leavitt of the *Emancipator* and Bailey of the *National Era*, defended the "one idea" course of the Liberty Party, though they as individuals reserved the right to express themselves on other issues. Leavitt opposed the organization of the Liberty League, but did not take issue with its doctrines.

Just as there was dissatisfaction with the Liberty Party platform, so was there discontent with its candidate. Birney had been an uninspiring leader in 1840; in 1842, Smith and others tried to get William H. Seward into the party, but failed. In 1843 Henry B. Stanton led protestors from Massachusetts who tried to get Judge William Jay of New York as a compromise candidate. Salmon P. Chase of Ohio was another leader of the group seeking a more expedient nomination; at an Ohio antislavery convention in December, 1841, he suggested John Quincy Adams or Seward. However, Eastern men like Smith and Leavitt were suspicious of Chase, a "raw recruit" who had voted for Harrison in 1840. Chase even wrote Birney, in January 1842, suggesting that Birney might find it wise to step down and allow another to be nominated in 1844. Birney replied that he would gladly comply if a suitable candidate could be found within Liberty Party ranks. He complained that Ohio was considering the opposition to slavery too much as economic policy, too little as religious duty.

Chase himself seemed to feel that the Liberty Party would best serve the country by forcing the Democratic Party into an Antislavery position. He was a Whig in

1840. In 1844 he thought the Liberty Party was a "real Democratic party . . . not in name only, but in deed and truth" that would make abolition only one great and necessary step in a broad program of reform. In 1846, he wrote to Joshua Giddings opposing Whig economic principles, and agreeing with the Democratic stand. Chase contended that the Democratic Party was far more likely than the Whig to take an antislavery stand, and the Liberty Party might well force it to do so.

James G. Birney had some rather curious views about democracy for one who was staking his success on the hustings. He was an aristocrat by nature, who had found Jacksonian democracy at the root of many evils. How, he asked, could people who censored mails, curtailed freedom of speech, unjustly treated Indians and Mormons, and maintained human slavery, be trusted to govern themselves? No doubt stung by the paucity of his votes in 1840, Birney, in accepting the party nomination for the 1844 election, stated that freedom, justice, and law were being sacrificed to the new god, Public Opinion. And Gamaliel Bailey, supporting a party seeking control of the national government, showed a strange distrust of the power of the government, and declared that between the states and the central government, his sympathies inclined to the former.

In preparation for 1844, the Liberty Party tried to organize on the local level, sought to control town and county offices, distribute campaign tracts, and establish committees of correspondence. Birney made a series of speaking tours in New England and his vote in the national election increased to 62,300. His vote in New York was larger than the plurality of James K. Polk over Henry Clay, and since that state's electoral vote gave the election to Polk, the Liberty Party claimed to have determined the outcome. Elections in Ohio showed a similar balance of power situation; in 1842, the Democratic candidate for Governor beat his Whig opponent by less than 4,000 votes, while Leicester King, the Liberty candidate, got 5,405 votes; in 1844, the Whig gubernatorial candidate won by 1,300 votes, with over 8,000 going to King.

After 1844, votes in state and local elections increased but little. The rising enthusiasm of 1841-1844 was lacking; the Liberty Party was beginning to realize its failure. In 1846, the party put forth its last great effort, and got its highest vote—74,017. During the same year in New York, the party made some gestures toward coalition with Whigs to select candidates to the State Constitutional Convention, and in New Hampshire Liberty men cooperated with Democrats to help send John P. Hale to the Senate. But from the banner year of 1846 the party fortunes steadily declined. After the introduction of the Wilmot Proviso in Congress in 1847, some Liberty men began to consider a merger with a broader antislavery movement organized on the basis of the proviso. Many Liberty men wanted to postpone their convention in order to try and take advantage of the budding Free-Soil sentiment; however, the party went ahead and held its own convention October 20, 1847, at Buffalo. At the convention delegates beat down attempts by Gerrit Smith to declare slavery unconstitutional in the states and to enlarge the party platform. Smith got 44 votes for presidential nominee, but was defeated by adherents of John P. Hale. Here the faction of expediency won a victory, for Hale was not a Liberty man, but an Antislavery Democrat. His nomination aroused much discontent in the East, but the West received it with favor.

The conflict in 1847 over the date of the Liberty convention was an omen of the breakup of the organization in 1848. In general, the western elements of the party wanted to postpone the convention until the strength of proviso sentiment could be measured, while Easterners demanded an early convention and nomination. After the party met and nominated Hale, the advocates of coalition with proviso men kept up their arguments. Bailey suggested that Hale should decline his nomination before the proposed Buffalo Free-Soil convention in August, 1848, so as not to prejudice its action. The American and Foreign Antislavery Society opposed any such coalition, insisting that the Liberty Party adhere to its candidate and platform, instead of accepting a subsidiary issue like territorial expansion.

Nevertheless, Liberty Party men, led by Chase, Stanton, and Leavitt, went to the Buffalo convention, where Chase wrote the platform, Stanton put Hale's name before the convention and then voted against him, and Leavitt moved that the nomination of Van Buren be made unanimous.

Leavitt's motion officially marked the death of the Liberty Party.

Free Soil. The larger third-party movement with which the Liberty Party merged was the Free Soil Party —a party which gathered many discontented groups into a momentary coalition committed to fight against the dominant Southern influence in both Democratic and Whig Parties. Their unifying device was the proviso which David Wilmot had added to an appropriations bill—that slavery should not exist in any territory acquired from Mexico. The Proviso angered the South and furnished a rallying point for all the South's opponents.

Prominent among the South's enemies were the supporters of Van Buren in New York, who were angered by the selection of Polk in 1844. When Polk gave the New York patronage to the Hunker faction, Van Burenites sought revenge. Polk's course stirred other discontents as well. In New England there was a demand for a higher tariff. In the Northwest men were dissatisfied with Polk for compromising with England over Oregon, his opposition to internal improvements, and his allocation of appointments to "Old Fogy" Democrats. From Missouri came the potent Blair family, prompted by personal animosity to Polk.

The dissatisfied Democrats of New York led the series of events producing the Free Soil Party. In New York there had long been a split between reforming Barnburners (like the Dutch farmer who burned his barn to get rid of the rats) and the Hunkers (who "hunkered" only for office.) In 1846, Silas Wright, Barnburner and Democratic nominee for Governor, lost the election, and Barnburners blamed the Hunkers for failing to support him. Though Van Buren's disappointment in 1844 did not create the Barnburner movement, his friends were able to take advantage of radical Barnburner opinion for their own ends. Van Buren adherents and regular Barnburners alike were opposed to Polk, his use of patronage, and what they felt was Southern dominance in the party; and they found the Wilmot proviso provided perfect ground for uniting. Organizing a Free-Soil movement would get revenge for Van Buren, destroy the enemies of Silas Wright, and cleanse the party of the dominance of Southerners. Free Soilers such as Preston King were not blind to the political potential in enlisting Van Buren and his supporters in their cause.

Thus, on September 29, 1847, the State Democratic Convention at Syracuse, New York, was stormy. The delegates split over adopting the Wilmot Proviso, and Barnburners left the convention. The Hunkers met January 26, 1848 at Albany and appointed a full delegation to represent the state at the National Democratic Convention in May; on February 16 the Barnburners held their own convention at Utica, and also appointed a full delegation to Baltimore. At the convention there was a great dispute over the seating of the rival New York delegations, and the Barnburners finally withdrew, calling another convention to make the "regular Democratic nomination." This convention was to meet at Utica, June 22.

The Utica convention turned up various opinions on the proper course for the schismatics. Some wanted the insurgents to make their own nominations, others disagreed. Finally, after deciding nominations were in order, the delegates (not all those attending were from New York —some came from Wisconsin, Ohio, Illinois, Massachusetts, and Connecticut) cast 69 votes for Van Buren, to 25 for all others, and the nomination was made unanimous. The convention then indicated its support for any national convention that might be called to unite the country on a Free-Soil basis. Such a convention had already been called by a People's Convention of Friends of Free Territory, which met in Columbus, June 20. After the Utica meeting, Democratic politicians, led by Van Buren's son, "Prince John," assembled at Albany and issued a call for a national Free Soil Convention at Buffalo on August 9, 1848.

For months the staunchest Antislavery leaders, certain neither Democrats nor Whigs would adopt a clear-cut platform and a satisfactory candidate, had been preparing for this occasion. Henry Wilson and Charles Allen, representing the "Conscience Whigs" of Massachusetts at the Whig National Convention June 7, 1848, walked out of the convention upon the nomination of Zachary Taylor. Such men as Charles Sumner, Horace Greeley, Schuyler Colfax, Chase, Giddings, and Charles Francis Adams had been busy seeking logical candidates and a common platform. Giddings, Adams, and Greeley hoped Thomas

Corwin of Ohio would be their standard-bearer. Other disgruntled Whigs liked Justice John McLean of Ohio. Liberty men, eyeing the growing proviso sentiment, hoped to see their own John P. Hale chosen to lead the new cause. But as the Barnburner revolt developed, the more realistic of the proviso men realized that their best chance lay with some Barnburner leader. Thus, when the Utica convention chose Van Buren, it virtually determined the later nomination at Buffalo. (*See Document No. 12.*)

New York Barnburners kept the Buffalo Convention well in hand. Liberty Party men came and were easily seduced by the smooth persuasiveness of the New York politicians. Joshua Leavitt later remarked that he had been quite impressed with the "tone of candour and respect which the friends of Mr. Van Buren exhibited towards Mr. Hale and the Liberty Party, and the utter absence of anything like attempts either to coax or coerce us to the support of their candidate." The convention itself was bedlam. Masses of people from all the New England and Middle States, the Northwest, and from Delaware, Maryland, Virginia, and the District of Columbia attended. Since there were too many to form any kind of efficient convention, it was agreed to let each state choose a number of delegates to form a Committee of Conference; this Committee transacted all the business while the majority sat in a big tent to hear speeches. It was a motley assembly; according to H. B. Stanton, pro-slavery Democrats were there to avenge Van Buren, Free-Soil Democrats to avenge Silas Wright; Henry Clay Whigs came to help strike down Taylor, and antislavery Whigs attended to venerate John Quincy Adams. Abolitionists attended, ranging in hue from the Free-Negro leader Frederick Douglass to Salmon P. Chase.

Western Liberty men were quite in evidence; their most important representative, Chase, headed the platform committee. The platform was a mélange of issues with bait for almost anyone who might read it. The Free Soilers pledged they would use the national government to discourage slavery, abolish it where possible (e.g. the District of Columbia), prohibit its extension, guarantee retrenchment, cheap postage, abolish unnecessary offices, create more elective offices, favor internal improvements, demand a homestead law, early payment of the public debt,

and a tariff for revenue. From the beginning, certain
Liberty men like Chase and Leavitt were ready to vote
for Van Buren instead of Hale if they got desired planks
in the platform. Apparently satisfied with the platform,
these men voted for Van Buren on the first ballot. The
final vote was 244 for Van Buren, 181 for Hale, 41 scattered. Leavitt then made an eloquent speech, buried the
Liberty Party, and moved the unanimous nomination of
Van Buren.

For Vice President, the Free Soilers (or Free Spoilers,
to use Webster's phrase) selected Charles Francis Adams.
This prompted William Lloyd Garrison to comment that
"When Van Buren and Charles Francis Adams combine,
the Revolution has at least begun." But Garrison also
perceived that the party was "a sign of discontent with
things political . . . reaching for something better . . .
It is a party for keeping Free Soil and not for setting men
free." Adams obviously had a hard time swallowing Van
Buren; he had once commented that Van Buren was fixed
to nothing but his own interests. His attitude illustrated
the hesitancy and doubt many New England Conscience
Whigs felt; men who, precipitated into existence by the
events of 1848, had little confidence in the success of the
Buffalo movement.

Many of the Democrats in the Free Soil movement
hoped that the effort would serve to put their own party
back on the right track. Wilmot, Chase, Blair, King, and
others all expressed the belief that they represented the
true Democracy, holding to the traditional doctrines. According to these men, Southern dictatorship had led part
of the party astray; it was up to them to light the way back
to true principles. Some Barnburners, like John A. Dix,
did not get so far away from the house of Hunkerism that
they had to take their feet from the door; Dix and many
others would re-enter the Democratic Party after 1848.
Others, including Preston King and David Wilmot, went
so far they had no choice but to seek refuge in the new
Republican Party. Likewise, Whigs like Giddings, Wilson,
and Adams cut themselves off from their old party. After
1848 such men only stood to benefit by continual agitation
of the slavery issue.

Though some Liberty papers choked on Van Buren,
they tried to unite behind the Free-Soil candidate. Bailey's

National Era led the way in proclaiming the dawn of a new day. Democratic papers were busy trying to cast calumny on Van Buren while keeping up a running fire on Taylor. The Washington *Union* called the Free Soil Party a gathering of Whig Abolitionists with whom no self-respecting Democrat, be he Hunker or Barnburner, would associate. The National *Intelligencer* pronounced the Buffalo meeting full of hypocrisy and insincerity, a device for party revenge that all honest advocates of Free Soil would avoid.

There were signs of failure in the months between the Buffalo convention and the election. In critical areas of the North and Northwest, Democrats and Whigs paraded their respective candidates, Lewis Cass and Zachary Taylor, as Free-Soil men. Many Whigs simply could not vote for their old enemy, Van Buren. Democrats sympathizing with the party voted, nevertheless, for Cass, convinced Van Buren could not win. Conscientious Liberty men recovered from their early infatuation and drew back. The national organization was weak and decentralized; there was not enough time to plan coordinated action; Van Buren was not a dynamic leader. In the election, Van Buren polled 291,263 votes, to Cass's 1,220,554 and Taylor's 1,360,999. Cass carried every Northwestern state.

After their defeat, party leaders disagreed about the future. Chase, continuing to hope the Democracy would be reformed, believed that "the Hunkers will require another defeat to bring them to their senses." He was ready to continue independent action; he warned Ben Butler of New York not to reunite with the Hunkers unless it was on Barnburners' terms. Gamaliel Bailey was already looking forward to the campaign of 1852, and pointed out that the 1848 election showed that the Free Soilers were strong enough in Ohio and Massachusetts to prevent an efficient organization of the Whig Party except on antislavery principles; the same was true of the Democratic Party in New York and Vermont. Thus, he said, the Free Soilers had the basis for victory in 1852, when they would either triumph at the polls or compel recognition of their principles.

For the moment, eyes turned to New York. There, a large Barnburner element wanted the Democratic Party reunited. John A. Dix and others were quite uncomfortable in a party containing Henry Clay Whigs and staunch abolitionists. It soon became clear that most of the New York Barnburners were going back into their old party. The Democratic rebels of 1848 supported Pierce in 1852 and Buchanan in 1856.

Collapse of the Free-Soil effort elsewhere sprang from the party's willingness to coalesce with the older parties. In Massachusetts the Free Soilers used their balance of power to combine with the Democrats, who were anxious to overthrow the Whig control in the State. The Free Soilers favoring coalition were led by Henry Wilson and Charles Sumner, while Adams and others opposed the move. In the 1850 elections the combination of Democrats and Free Soilers won a majority in the legislature. Then the chief purpose of this coalition came to light— the Democrats would help send a Free Soiler to the Senate, if the Free Soilers let the Democrats have the state offices. To the distress of the Democrats, their allies selected Charles Sumner for the Senate, but they reluctantly stood by their bargain and Sumner joined the growing anti-slavery contingent in Washington.

The tendency toward coalition in the Free-Soil Party was reflected in the Northwest. The old Liberty Party refused to combine with either of the old parties, but the new third party was filled with politicians who were impressed only by immediate gains. In Ohio, especially after the Democratic Party convention in 1848 adopted a free territory clause, the Free Soilers cooperated with them. The House of Representatives in Ohio had 32 Democrats, 30 Whigs, and 8 Free Soilers. Chase quickly began scheming for a Senate seat, in return for Free Soil votes for Democratic legislation. He finally succeeded—to the ruination of the Free-Soil Party, since Whig members condemned the action. In Michigan, strong personal antagonisms toward Lewis Cass aided a coalition between Whigs and Free Soilers.

The policy of coalition, which was poison to the party's future, did yield some immediate results; it sent Chase, Giddings, Sumner, Charles Durkee, George W. Julian, and others to Congress, and gave it enough power in Ohio to get a repeal of the Black Laws, and resolutions favoring the Wilmot Proviso. Coalition, and especially the Compromise of 1850, seemed finishing blows to the party. Yet in this year, 1850, when party affairs were at a low ebb, there was a return to first principles, and a reappearance of the religious, moral, and non-partisan slavery agitation. The new fugitive slave law produced an explosion. The old parties outdid themselves in getting rid of their Free-Soil doctrines to plant themselves on the Compromise. The Free Soilers proceeded to attack the Compromise, and in the Northwest, turned away from the "Free Soil" name to the title "Free Democracy."

In 1850 independent antislavery action pulled itself together and stood on its feet in every state again; the initiative came not from New England or New York but from the Northwest. A Cleveland meeting in 1851 had called a national convention to meet August 11, 1852 in Pittsburgh. This convention, which called itself the Free Soil Democratic Convention, had a more clear connection with the last Liberty convention in 1847 than with the Buffalo meeting of the Free Soilers in 1848. (*See Document No. 13.*) The meeting was enthusiastic; under the guidance of Giddings, the convention reported a platform based on the 1848 Buffalo platform, but with additional planks condemning the Compromise, the Fugitive Slave Bill, denouncing South Carolina's seamen laws, demanding recognition of Haiti, and stating that it was the duty of the United States government to protest against European monarchical intervention in countries trying to establish republican governments. One resolution also condemned any attempt to interfere with the privileges of property ownership and citizenship accorded to immigrants.

Salmon P. Chase lent his support to the convention, though he had been holding back until he saw the Democratic Party, by nominating Franklin Pierce, held forth no hope for an antislavery man. Chase hoped for a third party based on "Democratic principles" rather than a mere Free-Soil rally; he was quite disappointed when the convention failed to adopt the name "Independent Democracy."

The unanimous selection of John P. Hale as presidential nominee was a foregone conclusion; Julian of Indiana was his running mate. So recent was the party's revival that in the summer elections it did not receive a large vote. In Congressional nominations the party did not feel strong enough for much independent action, though there was more done in this area than in 1848 or 1850. In the Presidential election, Hale garnered 156,449 votes, to Pierce's 1,601,474, and Scott's 1,386,580. Despite the defeat, the Free Democrats, or Free Soilers, took heart at the signs of Whig collapse, and hoped for a share of these homeless voters. In 1853, the Free Democratic party in Ohio and Wisconsin—the only Northwestern states whose Free-Soil parties had maintained an unbroken existence, polled significant votes. In Ohio, Samuel Lewis won 50,346 votes as Free Democratic candidate for Governor, to 85,820 for the Whig candidate, and 147,663 for the Democrat. In Wisconsin, Whigs and Free Democrats produced a fusion ticket, running on the Maine Law under the party designation, "The People's Ticket." It lost the gubernatorial election, with 21, 886 votes to the winner's 30,405.

However, in no other state in the Northwest did the Free Democracy threaten the Whigs. Whigs would not enter *en masse* into Free Democratic ranks—union had to come about through a new organization. Agitators needed a new center of irritation around which a new party could crystallize. Eventually, the Kansas-Nebraska act offered a new opportunity.

— 5 —

PARTIES OF REFORM

Republicans. The passage of the Kansas-Nebraska Act in 1854 brought the sectional issues into a new focus and offered a new opportunity to unite the disgruntled elements of the country. Railroad interests in Wisconsin, foreseeing that the organization of Kansas Territory would interfere with their own schemes for a road to the Pacific with its eastern terminus in Milwaukee, assembled in Ripon, Wisconsin and called for all opponents of slavery extension, regardless of party, to unite. "Independent" parties in Illinois, Indiana, and Michigan, objecting to Democratic control and eager for internal improvements, launched candidates and campaigns. Unhappy Whigs and antislavery Know-Nothings in the East watched hopefully as the new groups, largely adopting the name "Republican," won successes. By 1856, politicians of many factions saw the opportunity to organize a new party. They assembled, first in a mass meeting in Pittsburgh on Washington's birthday and then in June at a nominating convention in Philadelphia, to form the new National Republican Party.

The Republicans were never a third party. They were, rather, the coalescence of third parties and fragments of old parties into a new major party. Free Soilers, Liberty men, Old Whigs, Know-Nothings, anti-Nebraska Democrats, Loco-Focos, Barnburners, and men whose political dissidence ran back even to Antimasonry came together, and in 1856 nominated John C. Frémont. The candidate's political experience was limited and his principles were unknown. Four years later they again rejected experienced leaders with pronounced principles to choose Abraham Lincoln. Thanks in part to a Democratic split Lincoln won the presidency and set about harmonizing the divergent interests and opinions in his amorphous party. The secession and Civil War gave the party a new issue and Lincoln succeeded, by compromise, patronage, and coercion, in unifying the Republicans and overwhelming their Democratic opponents. By the time of his death, however, he faced serious revolt from a Radical faction over issues of reconstructing the South. His successor, Andrew Johnson, fought and lost the struggle with the Radicals. Out of the long evolution the Republican Party emerged, by 1869 when Ulysses S. Grant became President, as a party of Big Business, the champion of railroads, national banks, and industries protected by a high tariff. "Big Business" dominated the politics of the later nineteenth century, and economic issues gave rise to sporadic protests and a succession of third parties.

The Democratic Dilemma. The Democratic Party's survival in the decades of Republican dominance constituted a minor political miracle. Serious rifts between Northern and Southern Democrats had been developing since Polk's administration and came to an open break when Stephen A. Douglas challenged the leadership of

President James Buchanan. In 1860 the party split, nominated two candidates, and went down to defeat. The next year, with the secession of the Confederate States, it lost its Southern members while many of its Northern adherents defected to the "Union" Republican Party. The remnant divided into Peace and War Democrats. Yet the margin between Republicans and Democrats was often narrow and despite bearing the stigma of "Copperheads" Democrats won sufficient successes in state and local elections to keep up a fitful existence. In the post-war years the party was rent by internal dissents which came into focus largely on economic issues. One faction, strong in the West, advocated paying the Civil War debts in greenbacks; Eastern interests, representing bankers and industrialists and laborers, abhorred fiat money and advocated a "sound" currency based on gold. When the Southern states were "redeemed" from Negro and Carpetbag rule, the new "Bourbons" of the South added their weight to the eastern faction. Local bosses in the West, often sharing patronage crumbs and frequently acting as agents for Eastern business interests, aided in keeping the Democratic Party from becoming a vehicle of protest. Until 1876 the Bourbons succeeded, often with difficulty and sometimes at the price of defeat in elections, in maintaining a party that was sound in finance and conservative on social problems.

The low point in the history of the Democratic Party came in 1872, when the party accepted the nominee of the Liberal Republicans. It was the only time in American political history that a major party adopted the presidential candidate of a third party. Only rarely did a third party agree to support the nominee of another, though the hope that a major party might endorse their candidates and platform continued to flicker in the minds of third-party promoters. Perhaps the experience of the Democrats with Horace Greeley effectively precluded any repetition of the experiment.

Liberal Republicans. The Liberal Republican movement was an effort to reform the Republican Party rather than to launch a third party. Not all the many elements in the Republican Party were happy over the victory of industrial and financial interests in the party's internal struggle. Low-tariff Westerners, civil-service reformers, and even business interests who foresaw that Republican reconstruction measures delayed economic recovery in the South were alike disappointed in the policies of the administration of Ulysses S. Grant.

Grant had offended many by his appointments to office —and many of his appointees were vulnerable to charges of corruption. In 1870, Carl Schurz, German-born Senator from Missouri, who had lost patronage when he incurred Grant's wrath, led a faction of St. Louis Radicals into a coalition with Democrats and the "Liberal"-Democrat combination carried the state. From Missouri the idea spread and in May, 1872, the anti-Grant soreheads, tariff reformers, currency experimenters, the opponents of centralization, and opponents of Radical Reconstruction assembled in a national convention in Cincinnati. There a group of newspaper editors—"Marse Henry" Watterson of the Louisville *Courier-Journal,* Murat Halstead of the Cincinnati *Commercial,* Samuel Bowles of the Springfield *Republican,* and Horace White of the Chicago *Tribune*— undertook to manage the convention in the traditional manner of "politicians in a smoke-filled room." Before the convention Salmon P. Chase, David Davis, Lyman Trumbull, Jacob D. Cox, Charles Francis Adams, and B. Gratz Brown had been mentioned as possible nominees. The self-appointed managers passed by each of these experienced leaders, and urged by Whitelaw Reid of the New York *Tribune,* gave the nomination to the *Tribune*'s editor, Horace Greeley. The platform was vague on protection, moderate on other reforms. The candidate's record as a high protectionist shocked the tariff reformers while his erratic career as sponsor of forlorn causes and aspirant for office amused observers. The reformers had surrendered their convictions to political expediency, stultifying themselves in hopes for a victory over U. S. Grant. The Democrats met and endorsed the Liberal-Republican ticket of Greeley and B. Gratz Brown. Late in the summer a "Straight-Out" group of Democrats met in Louisville and nominated Charles O'Connor. The nominee refused the honor, but on election day many a Democrat cast a protest vote for the Louisville nominee.

Prohibition. The Liberal-Republicans and the Straight-Out Democrats were two manifestations of discontent in 1872. Two other parties expressed two other forms of protest. Both the Prohibition Party and the National Labor Reform Party appeared on the scene. Both voiced long-standing grievances, and neither had any influence on the election. The Prohibition Party, however, did not fade from the scene. In election after election from 1872 to 1960, it doggedly ran candidates on platforms which advocated a wide range of radical reforms and pinned the blame for society's ills squarely upon the Demon Rum. (*See Document No. 14.*) In local politics temperance and prohibition men had occasionally exerted great influence: they had established prohibition in Maine, and Maine Law advocates had made headway in other states. Temperance groups had been important ingredients in the Republican Party. In years to come local option, statewide prohibition, and even national prohibition would be tried, but for none of these could the Prohibition Party claim credit. It was a peripheral phenomenon rather than the central agency of the temperance movement. James A. Black, its first nominee, polled but 5600 votes.

Labor. Like the Prohibition Party, the National Labor Reform Party found a single fountainhead for all the nation's evils: the money system seemed as bad to organized labor as the liquor traffic was to temperance men. In August, 1866, representatives of various trade assemblies met in Baltimore to form the National Labor Union. Promotion of an eight-hour day was the primary concern of the federation, and there was little that Congress or the national government could do about establishing working hours. The convention, however, decided to form a political party "as soon as possible." For a half dozen years the labor movement remained a local affair. In the meantime nearly all the leading trades tried to establish producers' cooperatives. In most cases the co-ops failed, but the experience brought the workers face to face with credit problems. Leaders and the labor press began to listen to the monetary theories of Western farmers who were demanding inflation of the currency. In 1867 the National Labor Union's convention attacked the national bank act as giving a money monopoly, and criticized land monopoly, but it made no move to launch a party. A labor party won some victories in elections to the Massachusetts legislature but failed to elect Wendell Phillips Governor. In 1870, with prosperity returning, there was a vigorous growth of trade unions, and an estrangement between the unions and the National Labor Union. As the bona-fide representatives of labor dropped out, the numbers of intellectuals and reformers in the membership increased. Claiming the union of all labor, and attacking money monopolies, the 1870 NLU Convention promised to form a National Labor Reform Party for the election of 1872.

In February, 1872, about 200 delegates met, adopted a platform calling for the government to issue more legal tender, pay the national debt in greenbacks, stop issuing tax-exempt bonds, reserve the public lands to actual home-steaders, and establish an eight-hour day. It favored amnesty for former Confederates and reform in the civil service.

As candidates the party considered Wendell Phillips, old abolitionist orator who was trying to play the same role in the labor movement that he had in the antislavery crusade; Supreme Court Justice David Davis who had been Lincoln's campaign manager at the Chicago Convention of 1860; old antislavery politician George W. Julian of Indiana, Missouri's Governor B. Gratz Brown, and Horace Greeley. Each of these was mentioned for the Liberal Republican nomination, and the labor politicians clearly hoped to select the man who could also be the Liberal Republican choice. Their guess fell upon Justice Davis—who waited until the Liberal Republicans passed him by and then refused the nomination. In August, the party placed Charles O'Connor, whom the Straight-Out Democrats had also chosen, at the head of their ticket. In November O'Connor garnered 29,489 votes. After this fiasco, the party struggled on as a state party for several years but made no other national appearance.

Greenback Parties. The 1872 experience with third parties, which might have discouraged politicians, stimulated third-party movements. The next year, panic hit the country and seemed to confirm all the charges which reformers were leveling at the economic system. In the midst of the depression the Greenback panacea took on new significance. For several years, in the Western states, farmers had been joining "Granges" of the Patrons of Husbandry—a semi-secret society devoted to betterment of rural social and cultural life. The Granges rapidly en-

tered politics and formed Independent Parties demanding
laws regulating railroad rates, opposing land grants to
corporations, and reform of banking taxation and civil
service. The parties paid little attention to Greenbacks.
They had some success, and succeeded in getting Grange
Laws regulating railroad and warehouse rates. The laws
met difficulties in the courts, however, and the Granger
movement declined. Only in Illinois and Indiana did the
Independent Parties survive, and here they were captured
by Greenback advocates. In 1874 the Indiana Independent
Party called for a national convention to prepare for the
elections of 1876. The convention, in the hands of Greenbackers, declared the money problem was the key question affecting the welfare of the people.

May 17, 1876, saw two hundred delegates, only three
of whom represented laboring groups, meet in Indianapolis
to launch the National Independent Party. The platform
demanded the repeal of the National Specie Resumption
Act and the issuance of United States notes. The delegates ignored a movement to run Judge Davis, and gave
their nomination to the aged Peter Cooper, New York
industrialist and philanthropist. The new party had no
funds, other than a donation from its candidate, and its
campaign was unaggressive. It had, however, a vigorous
worker in Marcus M. Pomeroy, one-time violent Copper-
head opponent of Lincoln, who organized thousands of
Greenback clubs and edited a Greenback paper in Chicago. The election gave the Greenbackers one per cent
of the popular votes—80,000.

The depression lasted past the 1876 election. Prices
and wages continued to fall. In the 1877 state elections,
Greenback tickets got from 5-15 per cent of the vote
from Massachusetts to Kansas. Probably the vote would
have been higher had not the major parties incorporated
part of the Greenback demands in their own platforms.
The state labor parties still in existence cooperated with
the Greenbackers, and in a convention in Toledo in February, 1878, the Labor Reformers and Greenbackers
merged. The platform contained labor demands on hours,
government labor bureaus, contract prison labor, and immigration; but the platform as a whole was a Greenback
document. It demanded fiat money—issued by the government to eliminate privileged classes. Other demands in-

cluded silver coinage, a graduated income tax, no tax exemptions for private property, and public lands for actual settlers.

In 1878 the Greenback movement reached its zenith, garnering over one million votes in state elections, two-thirds coming from the Middle West. In the East, too, the movement was primarily agrarian. The "National Greenback Party," as it was now known, sent 14 members to Congress, and elected varying numbers to the state legislatures. For the first time, independent politics also made a showing in the South.

In most cases the Greenback parties in the South sought alliance with the Republican machines, seeking the Negro vote. In 1878, Greenbackers got 56,900 votes in Texas, 61,000 in Missouri, 10 per cent of the vote in Tennessee and 22 per cent in Mississippi, sent 2 members to the Georgia state legislature, and elected 18 legislators in West Virginia. In Arkansas, fusion with Republicans sent 7 Republicans and 7 Greenbackers to the legislature. By 1882, the tactics of fusion swept the South; in Alabama, a fusion ticket got 41 per cent of the vote, and in South Carolina, 21 per cent; while the Arkansas Greenbackers, who abandoned fusion, got only 7 per cent. The course of the Greenbackers in Alabama was typical of the party's activity; here the guiding force was William Manning Lowe, a disillusioned Democrat who had failed to crack the party convention for a congressional nomination in 1878. Attacking the oligarchical organization of the Democratic machine, he ran as an Independent, using Greenback issues. The party organized in the state as a catchall for disaffected and discontented groups of all kinds; its fusion tactics ended with the Republicans in control, thus driving the Democrats back to their old party. Here as elsewhere, the Democratic charge of "race treason" was effective.

The Greenback party everywhere went downhill after the 1878 elections. The repeal of the Resumption Act right after the election took away one of the party's chief demands, and made the Democratic argument that more could be done through them than a third party seem plausible. More important in the Greenback decline was the renewal of industrial activity and the revival of the economy by 1880. The bonds uniting farmer and worker were broken, and the worker went back to attacking his employer, and the farmer to attacking the railroad corporation and the warehouse. Also, a rather severe fight over fusion weakened the internal structure of the party. As a general rule, the Greenback Clubs established by Pomeroy were the strongholds of those opposing fusion with the Democratic Party. In June, 1880, when the national Greenback convention met in Chicago, the Pomeroy wing demanded a distinct Greenback presidential candidate—and won, as the convention, after passing the usual planks, nominated General James B. Weaver of Iowa. (*See Document No. 15.*) Weaver played an active role in the campaign—he was the first presidential nominee ever to stump the nation. The results of the election gave Weaver 308,578 votes, less than one-third the 1878 Greenback vote. The party could not break the old party ties in a presidential election, though it could be somewhat successful in state elections, and it sent 8 members to Congress.

The 1880 vote indicated the indifference of wage earners to independent politics; the Greenback movement as it still existed was a movement of farmers. However, in turn, the Greenback propaganda, due to increased prosperity, was giving way to Anti-Monopoly agitation. By the middle of 1883, Anti-Monopoly sentiment was strong enough to call a national conference, though the Greenbackers generally opposed this movement. In 1884, the Anti-Monopoly Party held a convention in Chicago, passed various planks against monopolies, included some labor proposals, demanded election of U. S. Senators by direct vote, a graduated income tax, and appealed to the farmer to cooperate in the attempt to overthrow transportation, money, and communications monopolies. The convention nominated Benjamin F. Butler of Massachusetts on the first ballot. The Greenback Party met the same month in Indianapolis and after some dissension also nominated Butler. The millionaire lawyer waited till after the Democratic Convention, which nominated Cleveland, before he accepted the two third-party nominations. Butler's campaign lacked energy, and the vote was negligible—135,000, or 1.33% of the total (less than that polled by the prohibition candidate). A large section of the vote came from wage earners. The 1884 vote completed the process of dissolving the loose organization of elements that had been active in third-party politics since 1878.

The election of 1884 saw still another third party enter the lists. Unlike the other parties which were embodiments of economic dissents, the Equal Rights Party was primarily concerned with political liberty. For many years a determined body of women had been demanding the vote and the repeal of laws discriminating against their sex. In 1884 a group of suffragists formed their own party and nominated Mrs. Belva Lockwood, the first woman lawyer to practice before the Supreme Court, for the Presidency. Her scattered supporters cast but a few hundred votes, but in 1888 Mrs. Lockwood tried again.

Though the Greenback Party disappeared, the years 1884-88 saw other attempts to organize radical elements under labor leadership. In 1886, prompted by socialistic unions, Irish nationalists, single taxers, Greenbackers, and Anti-Monopolists, an independent political movement started in New York City. A series of disastrous strikes, court conviction of union members, anti-union legislation, and the activities of non-wage earning elements of the Knights of Labor all promoted this move. These various groups selected Henry George as mayoralty candidate; George lost to Abram Hewitt. He proceeded to take over the movement and organize it for his single-tax program, and drove the Socialists out of the party. In 1887, when the United Labor Party tried to run a state ticket and had no success, George withdrew from the movement. However, it was now completely infused with Single-Tax theorists, and meeting as a national convention in May 1888, with representatives from 10 other states, the Georgeites passed a platform favoring free trade and single tax, nominating Robert H. Cowdrey of Illinois for President, with W. H. T. Wakefield of Kansas as his running mate.

In 1886, Independent Labor Parties existed in many other states under various names, often working in close cooperation with the Knights of Labor. These parties also often included remnants of the Greenback Party, and farm organizations like the Agricultural Wheel of Arkansas, and the Farmers' Alliance of Texas. Socialists also supported the labor candidates. Each platform stressed

Labor demands, and most reiterated Greenback planks. The most common demand was for elimination of alien-land holding. The parties recorded good votes in Chicago and Milwaukee. Independent Greenback candidates everywhere fared worse than Labor candidates. In 1886, the Michigan United Labor Party got around 30,000 votes, and in Pennsylvania close to 17,000. In 1887, the Union Labor Party held a national convention at Cincinnati, with delegates from the Knights of Labor, Agricultural Wheel, Farmers' Alliance, Greenbackers, and Grangers. Of the 458 delegates at this meeting, the farmers distinctly predominated. There were no representatives of Eastern workers. The convention organized the National Union Labor Party, and chose an executive committee composed of farmers. However, the platform endorsed labor demands. At this time the Greenback Labor Party declared itself dissolved. Organized labor could not agree on whether it should merge with the new party or not; in the Middle West this was readily done, but merger was fought in the East. The New York United Labor Party wanted nothing to do with it, as the Union Labor platform had rejected the single tax.

By the autumn of 1887 the Independent movement was losing strength (*see Document No. 16.*), due to dissension in Independent Labor Party forces. The spring elections of 1888 were also disappointing, and it was clear the Socialists had withdrawn support from the Independent movement.

The Union Labor Party held only one nominating convention, May 15, 1888, at Cincinnati. The group nominated Anson J. Streeter of Illinois and Charles E. Cunningham of Arkansas for President and Vice President. The platform opposed land monopoly, contract and immigrant Chinese labor, favored peoples' ownership of transportation and communication, a graduated income tax, and direct election of Senators. The single-tax dominated United Labor Party met in convention at Cincinnati the next day, to nominate Cowdrey and Wakefield. After adopting a single-tax platform, and adding a few plans for government ownership of railroads and telegraphs and the Australian ballot, some members moved to merge with the Union Labor ticket; however, the Union Labor men wanted the whole United Labor ticket to withdraw,

and thus no agreement was reached. Eventually, the
United Labor Party withdrew from the contest, except
in New York, where it got a small, scattered vote. Streeter
got almost no votes in industrial centers, and totaled less
than 147,000 votes, the bulk coming from the West and
South.

The ineffectiveness of the sundry third-party movements
in the 1870's and 1880's might well have dismayed their
supporters had it not been for their occasional success in
state and local elections. Moreover, the continuous insurgency and constant turmoil in the ranks of both Republicans and Democrats, drove reformers to seek remedies
outside the major parties. Eventually, they hoped to find
a combination, even as the Republicans had once done,
which would bring a new party into power. As the nineteenth century entered its last decade, it seemed that
Populism might be the new, reforming party.

— 6 —

THE POPULISTS

"We meet in the midst of a nation brought to the verge
of moral, political and material ruin," read Ignatius Donnelly to the assembled delegates in St. Louis. "Corruption
dominates the ballot box, the legislatures, the Congress,
and touches even the ermine of the bench. The people
are demoralized . . . The fruits of the toil of millions
are boldly stolen to build up colossal fortunes, unprecedented in the history of the world, while their possessors despise the Republic and endanger liberty. From the
same prolific womb of governmental injustice we breed
the two great classes—paupers and millionaires . . . A
vast conspiracy against mankind has been organized on
two continents and is taking possession of the world. If
not met and overthrown at once it forebodes terrible social
convulsions, the destruction of civilization, or the estab-

lishment of an absolute despotism." (*See Document No. 17.*)

The time was late in February, 1892, and 800 delgates, representing 22 organizations of the "producers of the nation," had met to unite the "industrial forces" of the land. Important among the groups were the National Farmers Alliance and Industrial Union, the National Farmers Alliance, the National Colored Farmers Alliance and Co-operative Union, the Patrons of Industry, and the Knights of Labor. Their meeting was the third in a series which moved toward the organization—in July at Omaha—of the People's Party of the United States.

The Populist Party was the capstone of the demand for reform which had been growing in intensity since the Liberal Republicans and labor reform movements of 1872. For twenty years reformers had been protesting against the corrupt rule of Big Business, against the railroads, the national monopolies, trusts, high tariffs, the exploitation of labor, the national banking system with its resulting concentration of credit and finance in New York. Labor parties, Anti-Monopoly parties, various Granger and Greenback parties had severally voiced their protests. "Mugwumps" and "Independent" Republicans had supported reform candidates in the Republican Party or had switched over to support Democrats in local, state and even national elections. Scores of organizations—tariff-reform leagues, Single-Tax advocates, the Women's Christian Temperance Union, even a strange religious sect that proclaimed the earth was a hollow sphere—all asserting their abstention from politics, elaborated proposals for reform. It was, however, the movements among the farmers which brought the People's Party.

The Yeoman Tradition. The yeoman tradition in America was one which glorified the virtues of rural life and proclaimed that the farmers were the basic producers of national wealth. It was in no sense a peasant tradition of subsistence farming and social subservice. It was rather a memory of the sturdy independence of men who had stood firm at Crécy and Agincourt, at Lexington and Concord, Bunker Hill and Cowpens—of men who had followed the trails into the West and had hewn homesteads out of the wilderness. For the most part, the representatives of the yeoman tradition had been willing to

follow the political leadership of squires but had tested
the behavior of their leaders by criteria derived from the
soil. They demanded that public policy benefit the producers of the food and fabrics of the nation.

The economic transformation wrought by the Civil
War brought changes to American agriculture. The Homestead Act opened new areas of the West to settlement.
The grants to railroads threw still more land upon the
market. For a time after the war agriculture was prosperous, and prices were high. Southern cotton and Western
wheat enjoyed a boom. Agricultural machinery enabled
the farmers to cultivate more acres. Then late in the
seventies began a decade of good rainfall which led settlers to occupy normally arid lands. Expanding banking
operations made easy credit, and Western farmers borrowed extensively, mortgaging their property to buy more
acres, make improvements, and add machinery. In the
South a complex credit structure, centering in planter-
merchants and commission leases, with increasing tenancy
as a result, replaced the old slave plantations. Yet, the
readjustments brought hardships as well as prosperous
expansion. More and more the agricultural producer was
dependent, in selling his produce, on the railroads which
carried his crops to market, and on the banks which gave
him credit. He was the victim of high-interest rates, high
rates on the railroads and at the elevators, high prices for
the products of protected industries which he brought. In
time he suffered from overproduction, declining prices
in the world market, and drought.

The Alliances. The distress in Southern agriculture
brought a new organization to voice a protest and advocate reform. The Granger movement of the 1870's had
been weaker in the Southern states than in the Middle
West, and Greenback proposals made little headway. Yet
Southern producers found themselves impoverished by
forces which were binding them to a one-crop system.
Declining prices and mortgages caused much of the land
to fall into the hands of merchants and increased resentment against merchants and middlemen, manufacturers
and bankers, and the politicians whom they controlled.

In 1887 a defunct Texas Farmers Alliance was revived
by Dr. C. W. Macune and reorganized as the National
Farmers Alliance. Two years before, a Farmers Assembly

took form in Virginia, and an Agricultural Wheel began turning in Arkansas. The Texans were vigorous, sent out organizers, and within a couple of years had thousands of local lodges scattered throughout the South. In the beginning the Alliance proclaimed that it eschewed politics and was only a business organization. It prepared to distribute scientific agricultural information, establish cooperative marketing, and state "exchanges" for credit. Yet, the efforts of Alliance men met opposition from merchants and bankers, and they concluded that political activity offered the only solution to the farmer's ills. The Alliance advocated inflating the currency, destroying trusts and monopolies, regulating railroad rates, and repealing internal-revenue taxes. Later, it added a plan for a "subtreasury" which would issue warehouse certificates to circulate as legal tender. This was a political program, and Alliance men promptly went into politics. In 1888 and 1889 they captured the Democratic Party in one state after another and by 1890 had won control in North Carolina, South Carolina, Georgia, Texas, Arkansas, and Tennessee and had large influence in the Democratic Party in the other Southern states. Forty-four members of Congress, several senators, and the Governors of South Carolina, Texas, and Georgia were Alliance men.

In the meantime, a Northern Farmers Alliance developed in the Middle West. From the beginning the Northern Alliance had a political program, and attracted to it supporters of the older Greenback, Anti-Monopoly, and Union Labor Parties. More concerned with railroads than with marketing arrangements, they were advocates of government regulation and even ownership, demanded land reform, equalized taxation, free trade, and currency inflation. Their orators and their publicists shouted their hostility to finance capitalism and the money power, adhered to a labor-cost theory of wealth, and asserted a community of interest between rural and urban producers. Some of their ideas derived from Eastern radicalism, others harked back to the small-farmer ideal of Thomas Jefferson. They sought, in fact, to adjust the yeoman tradition to the problems created by corporate monopoly in an urban-industrial age. Their leaders were, for the most part, old third-party men: Ignatius Donnelly had been an original Republican, then a Liberal Republican, a

Granger, a Greenbacker, a Union Labor nominee for governor: Iowa's General James B. Weaver was a Republican who had turned Greenbacker; in Kansas "Sockless Jerry" Simpson was a one-time Greenbacker, a Single-Taxer, and a Union Laborite. As the Alliance movement spread, Alliance men formed third parties in the states, and late in the 1880's they won local offices and held the balance of power in several state legislatures. In 1890, Kansas Alliance men formed a "People's Party," won the lower house of the legislature, elected five Congressmen, and sent Editor William A. Peffer to the United States Senate.

The People's Party. In December, after the 1890 elections, the Southerners met at Ocala, Florida, to exult. To the meeting came agents of the Northern Alliance urging the formation of a third party. A few Southern leaders, notably Leonidas L. Polk, editor of a North Carolina farm paper, were agreeable, but most Southerners preferred to work in the Democratic Party. They agreed, however, to meet in Cincinnati in May, 1891. To the Cincinnati meeting came representatives of the Northern Alliance, a handful of Southerners, followers of Edward Bellamy who called themselves Nationalists, and a sprinkling of Henry George's Single-Tax men. The convention formally launched the People's Party and called for all the reform interests to meet in St. Louis in February, 1892. The St. Louis meeting adopted Donnelly's platform, and called for a nominating committee to meet in Omaha on the Fourth of July.

In Omaha nearly 1400 delegates, wild with enthusiasm, accepted most of the St. Louis platform with its rhetorical preamble, endorsed the free coinage of silver at a ratio of 16 to one, proposed that the per-capita circulation of money be increased to fifty dollars, advocated government ownership and operation of railroads, condemned alien ownership of lands, favored a graduated income tax, postal-savings banks, and a sub-treasury system. In the area of political reform they advocated the secret ballot, the initiative and referendum, direct election of senators, and a single term for the President and Vice President. For President the party nominated James B. Weaver, a Union veteran of the Civil War, and for Vice President General James G. Field, an ex-Confederate from Virginia.

The campaign began with vigor and General Weaver made a strenuous speaking tour. But it quickly became evident that the Southern Alliance men would stick with the Democratic Party. Although the Democratic Party renominated Grover Cleveland and ignored Alliance demands, the farmers were close to control in every Southern state. Leaders of the Alliance favored the third party, but South Carolina's Ben Tillman, Georgia's Tom Watson, and Texas' Jim Hogg refused to leave the Democrats. Local Populist organizations sought fusion with Republicans and made an appeal to Negro voters. The result was a marshaling of Bourbon forces, a revival of the intimidation, violence, and corruption which had once ousted the carpetbaggers, and in the end Alliance men, whether they wore the Republican or Democratic label, were defeated.

In the West, the third-party movement lost ground. In Kansas, Nebraska, and the Dakotas the Populists made headway, but in Minnesota the Republicans forestalled the new party by nominating a good Alliance man, Knute Nelson, for Governor. In the "silver" states of the Far West there was more interest in free silver than in the rest of the Populist program, and there the party made progress. In the end Weaver carried Kansas, Colorado, Idaho, and Nevada, and received one electoral vote in North Dakota and one in Oregon, for a total of 22 electoral votes. His popular vote was over a million in a total of nearly 12 million.

The showing was better than any previous third party had made, and it might well have encouraged greater efforts. But the appearance was deceiving. The campaign had weakened the Alliances and they were no longer able to furnish a base for the party. Southerners had not cooperated—partly because the interests of cotton producers and wheat farmers were not the same, partly because the Negro issue drove Southerners back into the Democratic ranks. The embattled farmers had failed to appeal to eastern laborers. (*See Document No. 18*). Moreover, they had attempted fusion locally—with Republicans in the South and with Democrats in the North—and their partners controlled the combinations. Perhaps, indeed, they might have overcome their difficulties had not the Panic of 1893 given a new emphasis to the money question and strengthened the demand for free silver.

The Populists had little enough chance to prove their ability. In few states did they control the legislatures. In Kansas, where Populism had its greatest strength a "legislative war" brought armed men to the state house and the party got few laws enacted. In other states Populists combined with other parties and enacted some purely Populist legislation. But most of their laws were either badly drawn or unconstitutional and the courts disallowed them. On the whole, the Populists made a poor showing.

Long before the 1896 election the Populist Party, like the Democratic, had been captured by the advocates of free silver, and the spirit of fusion had entered the ranks. When the People's Party met in June, 1896, the Democrats had already nominated William Jennings Bryan on a free-silver platform, and agents from the Democracy were present to propose fusion. Southern Populists opposed, alleging that the Democrats could not be trusted, but the delegates endorsed Bryan. To preserve the fiction of independence, however, they refused to accept the Democratic candidate for Vice President. They nominated Tom Watson of Georgia, and he carried on a lonely and hopeless campaign. In most states fusion tickets of Populist and Democratic parties appeared, but always the Democrats dominated the tickets.

The party died slowly, wrenched with internal dissension. In 1900 fusionists insisted on endorsing Bryan again, while pure party men hoped to revive the party and return it to its original principles. The fusionists won, and this time the separate Populist Vice-Presidential nominee withdrew. In 1904, and again in 1908 the remnants of the party chose candidates but their force was spent and their votes were few. Fusion had given the People's Party its death blow, but perhaps a returning prosperity was the basic factor in undermining the movement.

But even though Populism collapsed as a separate party, its influence was long lasting. The yeoman protest continued—partly as a result of fusion and partly because the panaceas of the Populists touched on basic problems— in both the major parties. Bryanism in the Democratic Party and La Follette Progressivism in Republican ranks both had their roots in Populism, and most of the demands of the Populist Party eventually became law.

THE BULL MOOSE PROGRESSIVES

Populism was a movement which gathered up sundry elements of discontent, proposals for reform, and theories of government. It was essentially, however, a political expression of the agrarian tradition in America and its ancestry ran back through a line of agitators for a Homestead Act, Antirent rioters, Antimasonic protestors, Jeffersonian frontiersmen, whiskey rebels, and the followers of Daniel Shays. And, although the People's Party failed, the traditions which it embodied extended into the future. Alliance men remained in the Democratic ranks, furnishing a number of Southern "progressive" governors, supporting William Jennings Bryan, and disconcerting Eastern bankers and old and conservative leaders. Among Republicans, Westerners and Midwesterners carried the memory of the Populist vote and advanced Populist programs and principles.

In addition to the agrarian protest, there were other reforming forces which stemmed from different concepts of government and, although often agreeing with the Populist-Progressive proponents on immediate programs, looked to different objectives. One such force, manifested in a score of groups, was socialism. Another, less given to theoretical ideology, was a reformism which reflected a middle-class morality horrified by corruption in politics and the corrupt alliance of Big Business and government.

Socialism. The Socialist movement in the United States combined both European Marxist—or "Scientific" Socialism and a native American Utopian Socialism. In the 1840's and 1850's sundry experiments in communal living—New Harmony and Brook Farm, for example—familiarized Americans with the social theories of early European and American Utopian Socialists. The collapse of most of the communities and the failure of others to do more than barely survive confirmed Americans in the belief that social experiments were impractical. In the years shortly after the Civil War, American labor, struggling toward organization, met newly imported forms of Socialism. In New York, German workingmen imported the different ideas of Karl Marx and Ferdinand Lassalle, and in 1868 the Lassallean German Workingmen's Union and the Marxist Communist Club united to form the Social Party of New York. In 1874 the Labor Party of Illinois polled nearly a thousand votes in Chicago. In 1876 the Illinois group, counting about 600 members united with the Social Democratic Workingman's Party of North America with 1800 members and the International Workingmen's Association—635 strong—to launch the Workingmen's Party of the United States. In the next few years the miniscule movement was rent by factions which differed both in general theory and in the practical question whether Socialists should work through labor unions or enter the political arena. Under various names —Socialist Labor Party, Progressive Labor Party—they held conventions, adopted platforms, ran candidates for local offices, were in and out of Henry George's single-tax movement, and sought leadership in the unions which entered the American Federation of Labor. Labor's rejection of political action convinced Socialists they had little to gain by trying to work through the trade unions.

In the early 1890's the popularity of Edward Bellamy's *Looking Backward* brought a new element into Socialism. Published in 1888, the novel pictured a society which was, substantially, Utopian Syndicalism with industrial production "nationalized." The proposals harked back to earlier native American radicalism, and their simple solution to the ills of the economic order had a wide middle-class appeal. "Nationalist" clubs spread the idea that government ownership and regulation was a workable solution for monopolies and trusts. In 1892 Nationalists appeared in strength at the Populist Party conventions, alarming Conservatives with their outspoken Socialist proposals.

Throughout the 1890's the Socialist Labor Party was under the thumb of Daniel De Leon who left the respectable, middle-class Nationalist Club movement. An attorney and a teacher in Columbia University, he became the party's national lecturer, and in 1891 polled nearly

15,000 votes as candidate for Governor of New York. He exerted influence in the Knights of Labor until he formed an independent Socialist Trade and Labor Alliance which won the jealous enmity of both the declining Knights and the rising American Federation of Labor. De Leon never succeeded in Americanizing the Socialist Labor Party or winning the labor movement. He was a doctrinaire Marxist, preaching class antagonisms, and excluding Christian Socialists, Fabians, Trade-Union Socialists, and groups which hoped to work with the Populist Party. (*See Document No. 19.*)

De Leon's and the Socialist Labor Party's failure gave opportunity to a new, more American, Socialist party. In 1897, Eugene V. Debs, president of the American Railway Union, organized the Social Democracy of America at the union's last convention. (*See Document No. 20.*) The party's declaration of principles stemmed out of the defunct Nationalist movement. After suffering from the same kind of growing pains as other left-wing movements—factional dissension, personal rivalries of leaders, violent disputation over policies—the party emerged, in 1901, as the Socialist Party of America. Its platform—handiwork of Marxist Victor Berger of Milwaukee—demanded complete governmental ownership of the means of production and distribution, and advocated independent political action and trade unionism. In 1900 Socialist candidate Debs polled 94,777 votes. Four years later, after still more internal confusion but with the accession of many liberals and intellectuals, Debs received 408,000. By the 1908 convention, representatives of the working class were a minority, while lawyers, small business men, editors, former politicians, and Protestant ministers dominated the party. That year the Socialists expected nearly a million votes, but in 1908 both Democrats and Republicans proclaimed their devotion to reform, and the A. F. of L. endorsed Bryan. Debs' vote increased only to 421,000. For four more years the Socialists worked. They made strong efforts to win immigrant votes, gave vigorous support to striking workers, and capitalized upon the failure of many reform organizations to satisfy a growing demand for economic and social opportunity. In 1910 the party vote reached 600,000 and Victor Berger won a seat in Congress. Local elections added to the strength in 1911, though most of the Socialists who won office were ministers or professional men who ran on reform issues crucial in their communities: local option, prohibition, corruption, graft, and extravagance in municipalities, boss and gang rule, and public improvements of schools, playgrounds and public health. For the most part they softened their attacks on capitalism. In 1912, the moderate, non-revolutionary reformism of the party gained Debs 900,000 votes.

Muckrakers and Reformers. In the two decades after the Populist Party's only independent campaign, other organizations besides the Socialists capitalized upon the need for reform. About the turn of the century a group of journalists began to point out instances of corruption in cities, states, and nation. Newspapers and popular magazines carried their stories. The *American Magazine, McClure's,* and *Everybody's* were new and vigorous magazines with wide appeal. In 1902 Ida M. Tarbell began relating the history of Standard Oil in *McClure's,* Thomas W. Lawrence exposed Amalgamated Copper in *Everybody's,* in 1905-06 Ray Stannard Baker put "The Railroads on Trial" in *McClure's.* The next year David G. Phillips writing in the *Cosmopolitan* on "The Treason of the Senate" showed that 75 of the 90 Senators served the railroads, the beef and sugar trusts, Standard Oil, and steel. Lincoln Steffens' "Shame of the Cities" and "Enemies of the Republic" showed the corruption in municipal and state governments. Samuel Hopkins Adams exposed patent medicines in *Collier's.* Other journalists and magazines dealt with banks, insurance companies, child labor, immoral traffic in women. They were, Theodore Roosevelt said, "Muckrakers" who were blind to the real glories of America. But the muckrakers claimed they were awakening the masses.

One result of the growing appreciation of the danger was a wave of reform and experimentation in city government. "Golden Rule" (Samuel M.) Jones and Brand Whitlock in Toledo, Tom Johnson in Cleveland, Ben Lindsey in Denver, and J. W. Folk in St. Louis fought corruption and reformed the administrations of their cities. In 1910 Emil Seidel, a Socialist, became Mayor of Milwaukee and began a long-lasting era of clean government. In addition to reforms, the cities experimented with new forms of government. After a flood in 1900, Galveston, Texas, emerged with a Commission replacing the old Mayor and Council. Staunton, Virginia, turned municipal affairs over to a City Manager. By 1912, over 200 cities had Commission Governments and many others were experimenting with Managers. Legislatures permitted cities to write their own charters, and the standards of municipal government rose.

La Follette Progressivism. The wave of municipal reform swept over into the states. J. W. Folk became Governor in Missouri, A. B. Cummings in Iowa, Hiram Johnson in California, and Charles E. Hughes in New York. Each fought the political bosses and the party-convention system which enabled the old-line-corrupt politicians to retain control. Each began to root out graft, sponsored corrupt-practices acts limiting the amounts candidates could spend on elections and restricted corporation contributions to campaign funds. Each sought to adopt devices—the initiative, the referendum, and the recall which might ensure popular control of legislation.

The reform movements in city and state had their greatest strength in the Middle West where Populism had prepared the way. For the most part, however, the reform movements were an expression of middle-class morality rather than of the yeoman tradition which the Alliances and Populism had represented. They rested upon journalistic exposures rather than upon a careful analysis of conditions. It remained for Robert M. La Follette and the Progressives of Wisconsin to find a sounder base for reform than mere indignation.

Populism had been weaker in Wisconsin than in other states of the Middle West, but the soil was right for political revolt. The state had been exploited by lumber barons, and the beginnings of reform came in a growing demand for conservation. A leading advocate of conservation was Charles Van Hise, President of the State University. The University of Wisconsin, too, had undertaken a program of agricultural extension by which it carried scientific information to the farming communities. In essence, the University was bringing science to bolster and enrich the yeoman tradition. The concept of public service, based on scholarly research, found a new expression as a group of social scientists in the University's Department of History and Political Economy began investigating social, economic, and political problems of the state. Faculty and graduate students probed into the workings of the credit structure, the transportation system, and the legislative process. It was a wedding of soil and seminar—the soil of the yeoman tradition and the seminar of the scholars—and from the union came substantial progress.

The political results became apparent when Robert M. La Follette, who had served three terms as a Republican Congressman before being defeated in 1890, quarrelled with and defied the Republican bosses of Wisconsin. For nearly a decade La Follette campaigned against "the system." His array of facts and his proposals for reform were solidly based upon research. In 1896 La Follette, leading a group of dissenters, announced himself a candidate for the Republican nomination for Governor. Defeated by the bought and controlled delegates to the convention, La Follette drafted a direct primary law and carried it to the electorate. In his campaign he carried his program to every part of the state, speaking on the dangers to representative government involved in the political convention and the powers of the bosses. For four years he campaigned, adding to his program demands for regulation of railroad rates. In 1901 he won the Governorship of Wisconsin.

The administration of La Follette consummated the wedding of soil and seminar. The Governor called in the professors to aid in launching a program of reform: together they elaborated devices to educate the people, and to create new governmental agencies for public purposes. Recognizing that trusts, big business, and even stalwart politicians could rely on expert advice in their activities, La Follette proposed to make the services of experts available to the public. Already the University's agricultural extension work had accustomed citizens to look to Madison for advice and leadership. La Follette extended the idea, and the functional-minded professors, already enlisted in La Follette's cause, were eager to serve. Governor and professors together erected doctoral dissertations into political institutions. Recognizing the power of money in politics, the Progressives passed corrupt-practices acts. Understanding the methods of boss-ridden conventions, they sponsored the direct primary. Confronted with the failure of elected officials to enact needed laws, they proposed the initiative and the referendum. Concerned with the waste of natural resources and the tendency of public lands to fall into the hands of monopolies, they adopted conservation measures. And, in order that there might be continuous study and constant watch, the Progressives created commissions, to be manned by experts, which would make recommendations to the peoples' agents. Charles McCarthy, Doctor of Philosophy, developed a Legislative Reference Library and assumed the task of drafting bills for legislators. Professor John R. Commons drafted labor legislation.

The methods of La Follette Progressivism, as McCarthy explained, were "a groping after and testing of one device after another . . . Patient research and care have been used everywhere." This was, in fact, the essence of Progressivism in Wisconsin, and the result was, according to Frederick C. Howe, to make Wisconsin into "an experiment station in politics, in social and industrial legislation, in the democratization of science and higher education. It is a statewide laboratory in which popular government is being tested in its reaction on people." The approach was pragmatic, yet in their governmental experimentation, the Progressives broke through the barrier which the Civil War had set up against the ancient libertarian doctrines of the rights of the states. The Progressives made no effort to integrate their philosophy with the abandoned constitutional dogmas of Jefferson and Calhoun, yet they were pragmatically reverting to the days when states had rights and were capable of assuming economic direction over the lives and activities of their citizens. The Progressive experiments were concrete efforts to reinstitute the lost rights of the states. Like the older, well-formulated doctrines of states rights, the pragmatic approach of the Progressives was justified and rationalized in the name of democracy. The Progressives never ceased to assert that government must remain in the hands of the people. They did not advocate, as did men of the Trustee tradition, that government knew best, and they did not create a state police to enforce governmental mandates. Social reforms without democracy were, in their opinion, an opiate for the people. They sought devices for widening the areas of democratic participation in government.

So long as La Follette remained in Wisconsin, the Progressive movement was oriented around state reforms, and around creating new democratic agencies of state government. But in 1907 La Follette went to the United States Senate, and thereafter his orientation was national. He assumed the leadership of other progressive-minded Senators from other Midwestern states, and undertook to apply the Wisconsin experience and experiments to the government of the nation.

In the meantime, while La Follette was bringing reforms in Wisconsin, Theodore Roosevelt was striking a reformist pose as President of the United States. A writer of note, an ardent imperialist, an enthusiastic commentator on public affairs, a self-promoted hero of the Spanish-American War, Roosevelt was a dramatic personality with a deep conviction that the Republican Party was the party of patriotism. He was a reformer because he believed the Republican Party should be cleaned from the inside, and because he saw that reformism might threaten Republican domination. He scorned Mugwumps, Independents in politics, and the "Goo-Goos" (Good Government League). In 1896 he found "all the men who pray for anarchy, or who believe in Socialism, and all the much larger number who want to strike down the well-to-do," together with "organized labor and the worst Unions" were voting for Bryan. Bryanism was, he concluded, "fundamentally an attack on civilization; an appeal to the torch."

As President, Roosevelt instituted prosecution of trusts, advocated regulating railroad rates, promoted conservation, and insisted on morality among public officials. This was, of course, reformism, but it did not touch the fundamentals of "the system" against which La Follette protested. It was, however, a threat to the stalwarts of the Republican Party, who breathed a sigh of relief when William Howard Taft assumed the Presidency. But the stalwart regimen met a continuing challenge from Progressives. In the House of Representatives, Midwestern heirs of Populism—Kansas' Victor Murdock and Nebraska's George W. Norris in the lead—launched an assault on the swollen authority of the Speaker of the House. In the Senate, La Follette marshalled Progressive Senators to challenge a new tariff measure. Reflecting something of the careful study which characterized Wisconsin Progressivism, each of the Senators made intensive study of some special schedule of the Payne-Aldrich Tariff, and brought to the floor of the Senate the results of their researches.

Out of the insurgent movement, in January 1911, came the National Progressive Republican League. Gathered in La Follette's Washington home, Progressive leaders—Congressmen, Senators, professors and publicists—adopted a program which would promote popular government and Progressive legislation. Specifically, the League stood for direct election of Senators, direct primaries for nominations, election of delegates to national nominating conventions, the initiative and referendum in the states, and effective corrupt practices acts. With this as his program, Senator La Follette began an active campaign to win the Republican nomination in 1912.

Theodore Roosevelt. In the meantime, Roosevelt returned to the United States from a hunting trip in Africa. He was distressed at the growth of insurgency in the Republican Party, and angered at Taft both because the President had seemed to depart from Roosevelt's program and because he had allowed a dangerous rift to develop in the party. For some months he refrained from comment while Eastern progressive leaders urged him to put himself at the head of the Progressive movement. Roosevelt inspired a group of Governors to invite his opinions, and replied to their inquiry with a vigorous endorsement of the terms in the Progressive League's program. At almost the same time, La Follette, worn out from long campaigning, made a rambling speech to an assembly of editors, and came to the verge of physical collapse. His momentary illness gave the 'practical' politicians of the Progressive movement an excuse for shifting their allegiance to Roosevelt. (*See Document No. 21.*) In a number of primaries, Republicans chose delegates to the nominating convention pledged to the ex-President.

In the Republican convention, Roosevelt delegations contested the seats of delegates pledged to Taft, and, when Taft men won control of the convention, a majority of the Roosevelt delegates refused to vote. A few hours after the Republican convention adjourned, the Roosevelt delegates who had been regularly chosen joined other delegations which had been denied seats, and in another convention nominated Roosevelt by acclamation as an independent candidate for the presidency. Roosevelt accepted, subject to ratification by a formal convention.

On August 6, almost 2000 delegates, paying their own expenses, met in Chicago in the convention of the Progressive Party of America. They assembled singing "Onward Christian Soldiers," lifted their voices in other hymns, and joined in the Lord's Prayer. Roosevelt arrived announcing that he felt "fit as a Bull Moose"—and the party had a candidate, a symbol, and a nickname. Amid scenes reminiscent of a religious revival, the convention adopted a platform favoring direct election of Senators, easier methods of amending the Constitution, woman suffrage, the recall of judicial decisions, minimum wages for women, prohibition of child labor, and inheritance tax and an income tax. There was confusion over the adoption of a plank regarding trusts and the final acceptance of a statement which was vague and evasive. La Follette and his followers, who refused to endorse Roosevelt or to attend the Bull Moose convention, charged that the anti-trust plank was concocted by George W. Perkins, a Morgan partner and a financial backer of Roosevelt, and that it revealed that Roosevelt was a political opportunist and no true Progressive.

Theodore Roosevelt was the third ex-President to lead a third party. Like Van Buren and Fillmore before him, his motive was partly revenge on the party which had deserted him, partly a forlorn hope to recover a past position of leadership. When the roll was called after the crusading enthusiasm of the Progressive convention had faded, it was seen that few of the older Progressives had followed the old leader. Only Hiram Johnson, who accepted the nomination for Vice President, remained among the Governors who had encouraged the movement. The only important senator was Albert Beveridge of Indiana. Instead of the Progressive office-holders, the prominent faces in the party were those of Perkins and Frank Munsey, the publisher of a line of Conservative newspapers. Basically, the leaders of the Bull Moose Party belonged in the tradition of the trustees—men of wealth who desired to make a goodly and godly society. Their concept of government was paternalistic. It was Munsey who told Roosevelt that

the government must "take on a more parental guardianship of the people." It should safeguard their investments,
their savings. "They need encouragement, the sustaining
and guiding hand of the state . . . It is the work of the
state to think for the people and plan for the people—to
teach them how to do, what to do, and to sustain them in
the doing." Lesser men in the party seemed to share the
same outlook. Many of them were prosperous business
men. They were men of the cities, with neither the viewpoint nor the background of La Follettists or Bryanites.
Few of them were experienced in politics.

The Bull Moose Progressives lacked the support of
local organizations and politicians. Hastily slapped together, the party never achieved a smoothly running organization. The Democrats nominated Woodrow Wilson, a
reform governor of New Jersey, and few Democrats supported Roosevelt. As a result, Roosevelt succeeded only in
defeating Taft. In the popular vote, the ex-President received 4,126,000 votes to Taft's 3,484,000, and won 88
electoral votes to Taft's 8. Wilson polled over six million
popular votes and had 435 in the electoral college. The
Progressives had become the second party in the nation.
Yet hardly was the election over when the party began to
disintegrate. In 1912 it had elected but one Governor and
barely more than a dozen Congressmen. Soon Munsey
began to advocate returning to the Republicans, while
other Roosevelt followers demanded that Perkins be dismissed. The factional quarrel weakened the party, and in
elections in 1914 the few Progressive office-holders suffered
defeats. Roosevelt began to search for ways to return to
the Republican Party. By 1915 he had decided that all
Republicans must concentrate their efforts on defeating
Wilson. The next year, the Progressives met in convention,
nominated Roosevelt again, and had their offer thrown
back in their faces. Roosevelt refused their nomination
and advised them to support Charles E. Hughes, the Republican nominee. The convention broke up amid tears of
anger and frustration, betrayed by its leader.

THE PROGRESSIVES OF 1924

The New Freedom. In 1912 Theodore Roosevelt called his program the New Nationalism. It was an appropriate description for its paternalistic concepts came more from Edward Bellamy and the Nationalist Clubs of the eighteen-nineties than from Populism and the Progressivism of Robert M. La Follette. Woodrow Wilson, who proclaimed himself the sponsor of the New Freedom, said Roosevelt's program would give a federal license to the juggernauts of big business to crush the American people.

The New Freedom, on the other hand, would place a fresh emphasis on the individual and restrict the federal government to the role of policeman and arbiter between the behemoth of Big Business and the citizen, the small business man, and the laborer. In 1912, Labor endorsed Wilson instead of Roosevelt, and the new administration was pledged to legislation which would benefit the workingman.

The Wilson regime began boldly. Wilson pictured himself as a British-type prime minister with a responsibility for legislation. On the day of his inauguration he called Congress into special session to consider the tariff. Weeks of debate produced the Underwood-Simmons Tariff with lower rates and including a graduated income tax. Then Wilson led Congress to deal with the banking structure and the result was the Federal Reserve System which brought the control of credit into the government's hands. After that came the Clayton Anti-trust Act and a Federal Trade Commission Act. With these measures Wilson appeared content—the New Freedom had eliminated some of the more glaring evils in the nation, and restored some business to free competition without having unsettled the economy or encouraged social disorder. Most of the legislation had been sponsored and guided through Congress by Southern conservatives.

But there were progressives in the Middle West and in Congress who wanted more drastic measures. Wilson opposed woman's suffrage, objected to federal land banks which would ease credit to farmers, and he thought a bill regulating child labor was unconstitutional. Once he had described himself as a "Progressive with the brakes on," and he now attempted to apply the brakes to agrarian reforms. But, as 1916 approached, it appeared that Roosevelt's Progressive Party was disintegrating and victory for a reunited Republican Party was possible. Mindful of the need for haste, progressive Democrats took the lead in putting through laws which would appeal to labor and farmers. Congress passed, and Wilson ruefully signed, a Federal Farm Loan Act, and others regulating grain elevators and the grading of grain, a Workman's Compensation Act, a law improving working conditions of seamen, an eight-hour day for railroad employees, and acts to aid agricultural and vocational education. When these measures were all on the statute books, Wilson entered the 1916 campaign boasting that he had carried out both the Democratic and the Progressive platforms.

The development of the New Freedom into a combination with the New Nationalism went on against a background of a war in Europe and a growing concern of Americans with foreign affairs. Steadily for three decades, the Eastern, urban "progressives," in full accord with the tradition of the trustees, had been asserting an American responsibility to make the world, as well as the United States, into a good and godly place. In the 1890's Josiah Strong, proponent of the Social Gospel, proclaimed the responsibility of the American branch of the Anglo-Saxon "race"—a new Chosen People—to extend Christ's Kingdom over the earth. The doctrine pleased both business interests anxious to exploit foreign markets and those who believed that expansion of trade was necessary to a capitalist economy. Politicians translated the religious and economic arguments into a program of expansion. William McKinley found a moral obligation to possess, Christianize, and civilize the Philippines. Theodore Roosevelt wielded a "Big Stick" over Latin America to inculcate the moral lesson that small nations should pay their debts.

Woodrow Wilson intervened in the Caribbean, in Central America, and in Mexico in the name of liberty and moral principles. When war came in Europe, Wilson proclaimed American neutrality, but as events progressed, he concluded that the Germans and the Axis Powers were violating moral standards more than Britain and her Allies. He steered a narrow course between the belligerents until after the election of 1916—which he won narrowly with the aid of the slogan "He kept us out of war"—and then moved quickly to take the country into the conflict on the side of "democracy," "the rights and liberties" of small nations. "America is privileged," he told Congress as he asked for a declaration of war against Germany, "to spend her blood and her might for the principles that gave her birth and happiness and the peace which she has treasured."

Socialists. Throughout these years of the New Freedom, the New Nationalism, and the crusade for international morality, two groups in America made political protests. Neither the La Follette Progressives nor the Debs Socialists were content with Rooseveltian morality and Wilsonian idealism. Although their criticisms of specific items were often couched in the same vocabulary, they sprang from different orientations, different traditions, different concepts of society, and different programs for reform. La Follette and his followers, oriented toward agricultural production, found that the New Freedom only strengthened the controls which financial and industrial corporations held over society. The Socialists, continuously torn by internal controversy, by "splinter" movements, by conflicts between foreign working groups and native American middle-class radicals, made the basic criticism of both Roosevelt and Wilson that their programs were mere reforms that left the capitalist structure untouched.

By 1912 the Socialists had grown in strength until the party had 150,000 dues paying members and a voting strength of 900,000. It had inherited voters from the Populists and was a serious factor in Texas, Oklahoma, Colorado, Nebraska, and Kansas. It was especially articulate in lower Manhattan, and in Milwaukee an alliance with trade unions gave it a Mayor, a Congressman, and sent Socialists to the legislature in Madison. Within their ranks were recent immigrants and Mayflower descendants,

sharecroppers and landlords, trade unionists, and tenement
dwellers—but an increasing number were intellectuals,
ministers, professors, and journalists, and the control of
the movement and of the party was tending to pass into
the hands of the middle-class representatives until it came
to appear only the left wing of the Progressives. In 1913
an internal doctrinal fight led to the expulsion of "Big
Bill" Haywood and a group of actionist revolutionaries
who advocated sabotage in industrial disputes. Within four
months the membership dropped to 40,000, and its middle-class character became more pronounced with the
victory of the Morris Hillquit-Victor Berger factions.

The legislation of the New Freedom had little Socialist
endorsement. Although the Socialists had long urged an
income tax, they found little satisfaction in the Wilsonian
tariff. The Federal Reserve Act seemed only a means of
strengthening the bankers' hold on the worker's throat.
The Clayton Anti-Trust Act exempted labor unions from
the restrictions placed upon other combinations in re-
straint of trade, but the Socialists were quick to notice
that this was no "Magna Charta" for Labor—as the American Federation of Labor hailed it—and that the courts
continued to enjoin strikers and accorded labor no privileges.

But it was foreign affairs which disturbed the Socialists
the most. The Socialist Party opposed the war in Europe,
and severed its connection with the Second International
because it had not taken steps to stop the war. Despite the
advice from American Socialists and from European leaders to stop the war by calling a general strike, German
Socialists rallied behind the German war effort and French
and English Socialists gave support to their governments.
In the United States the Socialists bent their efforts to
preventing the American government from entering the
war rather than attempting to end the war in Europe. On
the other hand, the Socialists, believing that the war was a
businessman's war, found it difficult to work with religious
pacifists and peace societies in the United States.

In 1916, the Socialist Party made a poor showing in the
election. (*See Document No. 22.*) That year, the right-
wing faction controlling the party selected Allan Benson, a
conservative, instead of Eugene Debs for the Presidential
nomination. Benson turned out to be an uninspiring leader,

while the expulsion of the Haywood Syndicalists and the
defection of others to Wilson and the New Freedom, cost
the party votes. Benson polled but 585,000—a third less
than Debs had received four years before.

In 1917, as the United States entered the First World
War, the Socialists assembled in St. Louis to declare their
opposition. The delegates to St. Louis were middle-class,
native-born Americans, and they voted, three to one, for
resolutions calling American entry into the war a criminal
act, pronouncing the war a capitalist conflict, and calling
for Socialists to resist conscription. The result was another
secession. A group of pro-war Socialists, mostly intellectuals whose articulateness made them seem more powerful
than they were, left the party and organized the Social
Democratic League of America. Through the summer of
1917 the League, with Charles A. Beard as one of its
leaders, tried to unite with the remnants of the Progressive
Party, the Prohibition Party, and woman suffragists. In
October they formed the National Party.

The new Nationalists proved ineffective—except as a
bridge for some Socialists to cross over to the Democrats.
The anti-war position of the Socialists proved an element
of strength. In the fall of 1917 Morris Hillquit, running
for Mayor of New York, polled nearly 150,000 votes—
surpassing all previous Socialist returns in the city.
Throughout the country, Socialists won more elections
and the party's vote increased.

The opposition to the government brought the full force
of governmental and mob action down upon the Socialists.
Patriotic organizations denounced the Socialists and encouraged mobs and local law officers to proceed against
them. Seven states passed laws abridging freedom of
speech, assembly, and the press. Congress passed an
Espionage Act, with enforcement and informers working
through the Post Office. The Postmaster General denied
Socialist papers the use of the mails. In Oklahoma the
Appeal to Reason defected to the war, and the party,
blamed incorrectly for sponsoring the Green Corn Rebellion—the only organized and militant protest against the
war—collapsed. Then, Debs, seized after he delivered
an anti-war speech in Canton, Ohio, went to prison with a
ten-year sentence.

Despite the hostility of the government and the imprisonment of the party's leaders, the Socialists kept much of their strength. The continued attacks of Germany on the Russians after the revolution caused many Socialists to urge a vigorous prosecution of the war. A meeting of the national executive committee in St. Louis in 1918 produced only a sharp clash between right and left forces— and yet the membership declined only from 83,000 to 74,755 in 1918. The next year saw an actual increase—but the party was impotent, its press muzzled, its leaders jailed. It was weakened by internal strife, its relations with organized labor were strained, and it had won the active hostility of large elements of the public which had hitherto been sympathetic.

The end of the war brought no diminution in the anti-Socialist campaign of the government. The new American Legion stirred up anti-radical hysteria, and the United States Attorney-General A. Mitchell Palmer launched fresh legal assaults on the party. Congress refused to seat Victor Berger in 1919, and refused again after his Milwaukee constituency sent him back to Washington.

The government's repressive measures brought reaction in favor of the Socialists, and many Progressives sympathized with their demand for amnesty for political prisoners. The party nominated Debs again for the presidency, and in 1920 the candidate, still in Atlanta Penitentiary, polled 915,000 votes—the largest number a Socialist ever won, but a smaller percentage of the total vote than in 1912.

Whatever sympathy the Socialists won was dissipated when the party once again suffered internal dissension and splintering. Revolutionary and evolutionary Socialists had lived together in precarious harmony, but now the left wing came to believe that revolution was imminent in America. Most of the left wing came from foreign groups —the language federations—and in 1919 the executive committee, composed largely of right wing "evolutionists," expelled the language federations and the Michigan Socialist Party. These soon formed their own organization, grew closer to militant Russian Socialists, and emerged as the Communist Party. Thereafter, the remaining Socialists spent much of their time and effort in fighting the Communists—though in doing so they themselves became more radical and drew away from traditional native American radicalism. The swing to the left alienated more conservative American dissenters from the social order. Western agrarian Socialists went into new farmer movements, while Eastern urban Socialists moved to the progressive Democrats, and sought fusion with progressive groups. In 1922 Socialists met in Chicago with representatives of the railway brotherhoods, labor unions, a Farmer-Labor party of Minnesota, church groups, and the inconsolable remnants of the Bull Moose movement. They joined the Conference for Progressive Political Action, and in 1924 endorsed Robert M. La Follette's independent candidacy for the presidency. Although they performed useful service for La Follette, their local and state campaigns suffered, and the Socialists emerged from the 1924 election weaker than ever.

La Follette. Throughout the years of the New Freedom and the World War, while the Socialists were valiantly trying and failing to make an effective protest, Robert M. La Follette and the Wisconsin Progressive Republicans were becoming increasingly hostile to Woodrow Wilson and his conduct of the government. In 1912 La Follette refused to support Theodore Roosevelt. "His whole record demonstrates," said *La Follette's Weekly Magazine,* "that he has no constructive power." He was a Progressive only in words, always ready to compromise in order to win. "He will not last. In the end the people of the country will get his true measure." La Follette Republicans carried Wisconsin, but gave the state's electoral vote to Woodrow Wilson.

In the legislation of the New Freedom, La Follette and the insurgent Republicans allied themselves with the liberal Democrats. Unlike Eastern "progressives" who believed essentially—for all their protestations of "pragmatism"—in the desirability of strengthening state power and increasing the government's role in guiding, regulating, and controlling individuals and society, the Populist-Progressives were interested only in the creation of new agencies for expressing the popular will and in eliminating the evils of the economic order. There was little theoretical underpinning for the Mid-Western "progressive" heirs of Populism: they believed that government should more fully represent the will of the people. Their orators and publicists concerned themselves with problems of making democracy work and of making government work for the people. In Wisconsin they had added the concept that research and experimentation could find the solution to problems—that the people could learn the truth, and that the knowledge would make them free. Yet, on the national level, La Follette and his followers were willing enough to adopt the specific reforms of the New Freedom. Their only criticisms came when Wilson seemed willing to stop short of complete reform. They joined with liberal Democrats in forcing Wilson to accept a child-labor law, a farm-loan-bank system, and extensive aids to agricultural education.

From the beginning, however, the La Follette Progressives were critical of Wilson's foreign policy. When the World War broke out, they endorsed neutrality, but joined with Socialists in pointing out that economic rivalries lay at the base of the conflict. When American business interests became involved, the La Folletteites exposed, step by step, their efforts to promote American intervention. When the Navy League screamed for preparedness, La Follette's magazine declared the League was "little more than a branch office of the house of J. P. Morgan and Company, and a general-sales-promotion bureau for the various armor and munitions industry." So, too, when Wilson, involved with Mexico, massed militia on the Mexican border and sent a punitive expedition into Mexico, La Follette unerringly scented oil and industrial interests.

In 1916, Senator La Follette announced his candidacy for the Republican presidential nomination. He denounced J. P. Morgan and "his dollar-scarred heroes of the Navy League," advocated nationalization of the munitions industry, proposed an embargo on arms and ammunition, supported a conference of nations to settle issues and an international tribunal for settling international disputes, and a popular referendum on any declaration of war. Wisconsin and North Dakota delegates to the Republican convention presented a platform calling for a scientific tariff, a patent law that would not foster monopolies, stronger pure food laws, government manufacture of munitions, strict neutrality, a conference of neutral nations, an international-peace tribunal, a referendum on war, the end of secret diplomacy and of dollar diplomacy, and woman suffrage. The Republican Party, nominating

Charles E. Hughes and concerned with enticing the Bull Moose rebels back into the party, ignored La Follette's candidacy and his proposals.

When, after his re-election, Wilson moved quickly toward war, La Follette became one of the "little group of willful men" who opposed Wilson's proposal to arm merchant vessels—a request, said La Follette, for "extraordinary and unconstitutional powers, to bring on war at his discretion." As the war came, La Follette began to talk at length about executive usurpation, on corruption, on the necessity of making war profiteers pay their share of war costs, and, above all, on the right of free speech. Through his magazine, which grew in circulation, the Senator exposed the munitions makers, the bankers, the steel trusts and the railroads, and carried on a running fight against the militarists, and the National Security League which would suppress free speech. His paper watched with interest the development of the Russian revolution, applauded Russian efforts at reform, and condemned Wilson's "private war" against the Soviets.

Eventually, bit by bit, a synthesis emerged from the mingled expositions and exposures: Big Business, operating through the "System" had permeated government in the United States. The people, operating through the Progressives and the insurgents, had been on the verge of restoring government to the people. Skillfully, the managers of Big Business and the "System" had backed Theodore Roosevelt to crush Progressivism, and elect Wilson. Then, partly to secure profits and partly to suppress Progressive criticism, the forces of monopoly had combined with militarists and jingoes and corrupt politicians to bring American participation in the war. Wilson went to Paris, abandoned the idealism he had voiced in his Fourteen Points at the beginning of the war, and came back with a "League of Damnations"—a victor's vengeful peace which would make the world safe for American monopolists, imperialists, and militarists but not for democracy.

The Progressive Party. Steadily the La Follette viewpoint gained attention. Revisionist historians began to reexamine the course of recent history. The subscription list to *La Follette's Magazine* grew. In the Senate La Follette thundered alternately against the League of Nations and the Esch-Cummings Railroad Act which would turn the railroads, taken over by the government during the war, back to private hands. By the beginning of 1920, the Senator could assert that "people were beginning to see that the war was fermented to feed the avaricious few." Thereupon, he launched a new move to secure the Republican nomination. A Committee of Forty-eight, seeing monopoly as the major foe, had met in St. Louis in December 1917. (*See Document No. 23.*) Until the Republicans met in 1920 it kept up an agitation, but the party's convention again would not even permit the reading of the Wisconsin platform. It nominated Warren G. Harding.

For two more years, while the Harding administration carried the country "back to normalcy," La Follette kept up the fight. By 1922 the vigorous campaign to instruct and arouse the voters began to bear fruit. In February, 1922, representatives from railroad brotherhoods, the Farmer-Labor Party of Minnesota, the Farmers' Union, the Nonpartisan League, the Church League for Industrial Democracy, and Catholic and Methodist welfare groups met in Chicago and formed the Conference for Progressive Political Action (CPPA). In November La Follette called for Progressives in Congress to unite, and in December they formed the People's Legislative Service dedicated to driving "Special Privilege out of control of the government and restore it to the people." In the congressional elections of 1922, "La Follette radicals" won a number of seats, and in the next Congress they acted as a group. They forced a raise in a surtax on incomes, prevented the government giving the Muscle Shoals power plant on the Tennessee River to Henry Ford, and attacked the Interstate Commerce Commission's favoritism to railroads.

In 1924, as in previous presidential years, La Follette announced his candidacy for the presidency. But this time, he announced as an Independent. The Republicans, as in the past, ignored La Follette and the CPPA's platform. They nominated Calvin Coolidge, and the Democrats, torn by sectional issues, eventually selected John W. Davis with Charles Bryan, brother of their one-time leader, for Vice President. Thereupon the CPPA met at Cleveland and endorsed La Follette. The Senator chose Senator Burton Wheeler of Montana, a Democrat who had won attention by investigating scandals of the Harding administration, as his running mate. La Follette, too, wrote the platform. "The great issue before the American people today is the control of government and industry by private monopoly," he began. He demanded a complete housecleaning in the executive departments, insisted that the government's power should be used to crush, not foster, monopolies. He favored public ownership of railroads, government development of Muscle Shoals, increase in the upper brackets of the income tax, a lower tariff, popular election of the President and of federal judges. The platform denounced war, imperialism, and militarism.

La Follette's candidacy and his platform received endorsement from the Socialists, who made no nominations of their own. The railroad brotherhoods gave their approval, and the national executive committee of the American Federation of Labor gave their "personal and non-partisan" endorsement. Moreover, they promised money for the Progressive campaign. They promised three million —they eventually contributed $25,000.

The Progressive campaign was conducted under insuperable odds. The Socialist endorsement enabled conservative Democrats and Republicans alike to attack La Follette as a radical. The Progressives lacked local organization and in many states La Follette's name appeared under the Socialist label on the ballots. The failure of organized labor to give adequate support was costly, and even Mid-Western farmers lost interest in the ticket. In the end, it was almost a one-man campaign, and La Follette's ablest and hardest working helpers were his two sons, "Young Bob" and "Phil." And yet, despite the obstacles, in November he polled almost 5,000,000 votes— nearly 17 per cent of the total cast in the election—and won the 13 electoral votes of Wisconsin. (*See Document No. 24.*)

The collapse of the Progressive Party after the election came suddenly. La Follette had, in fact, chosen the wrong year to run for the presidency. He might, indeed, have done better in 1920. By 1924 the country was prosperous, and after the corruption of the Harding years, it was under the conservative but honest administration of Calvin Coolidge. Hardly had the returns been counted when the Railroad brotherhoods withdrew from the CPPA. During the campaign Labor leader Samuel Gompers had grown cautious and come to regret his departure from Labor's avowed non-partisan stand. Labor organizations busied themselves making peace with the old parties. As the Socialists counted the votes—claiming to have brought one million to the La Follette total—they insisted on moving toward a new party. In February a conference in Chicago brought together Socialists who wanted new dynamic political actions, unions who wished to return to non-partisanship, and Northwestern progressives who wanted a new party but who were suspicious of the Socialists. The meeting ended in dissent, and the Conference for Progressive Political Action came to an end. To the division of council was added the loss of the leader. In June, 1925, La Follette, worn out from his strenuous efforts, died. He had been the single unifying element in a diverse and heterogeneous movement.

— 9 —

IN DIRECTIONS LEFT

For two dozen years after the collapse of La Follette Progressivism, the American political scene was devoid of an important third-party movement. Election after election showed Prohibitionists doggedly naming presidential candidates and increasing their vote from 57,520 in 1924 to 103,216 in 1948. There was an American Party, pledged to the principles of the Ku Klux Klan, in 1920 and 1924, and a Commonwealth Party which polled 1500 votes in 1924 and combined with the Prohibitionists in 1936. At various times and in scattered places a Liberty Party, a Social Justice Party, and a Farmer-Labor Party appeared on the ballots, while the Socialist-Communist complex proliferated with Socialist Labor, Industrial Labor, Industrial Government, Socialist Workers, and Militant Workers Parties. A few of the parties showed persistence but they had no appeal to masses of voters.

The period was one of unusual political turmoil and partisan bitterness. A larger percentage of the eligible voters went to the polls and there was a heightened popular attention to politics. But the voters cast their ballots overwhelmingly for the Democratic and the Republican candidates. The issues grew out of the Great Depression, the New Deal's panaceas for economic and social problems, and World War II. The voters chose between the programs and personalities of the major parties with little heed to the alternatives offered by the lesser groups.

Yet, in this second quarter of the twentieth century there were significant developments among the third parties. There was the decline of the Socialist Party, the rise and decline of Communism, a futile effort to form a right-wing party, an equally abortive attempt to revive La Folletism, and the development of satellite parties within the major parties. And eventually there was a final effort to establish a New Progressive Party. Perhaps, indeed, the major significance of the various third-party movements was the reaffirmation of the techniques of compromise and conciliation which enabled the old parties to survive.

Norman Thomas and the Socialists. Compromise between contending factions, and the harmonizing of often discordant interests were the basic means by which both Democratic and Republican Parties preserved their unity. The failure of the Republicans to incorporate the La Follette protest in their program and to make conciliatory adjustments to the Progressives had led to the La Follette revolt, but after 1924 the party made efforts to woo the dissenters back into the ranks. The withdrawal of Coolidge, and the concentration of attention on Herbert Hoover, a Progressive with a reputation for humanitarianism, brought most of the La Follette supporters back into the party. The failure of the Socialists to imitate the Republicans, resolve their internal dissents, and present a nominally unified front, accounted in no small measure for their lack of electoral success. Perhaps, indeed, the very nature of the movement prevented the kind of compromise that the other parties could make. The Socialists, in fact, never really determined whether they were a revolutionary sect, a political party, or a pressure group. They avoided showing concern with local issues, and in consequence—except for Milwaukee, Bridgeport, Connecticut, and a few other cities—they failed to build strong local organizations. They hoped, instead, to use labor unions in place of "grass roots" political organizations, and they failed to win Labor's support. Their language tended to be doctrinaire, deriving from Marxist jargon rather than the vocabulary of basic American traditions. American labor had little class consciousness; the American worker was still an individualist, and the American voter was more concerned with pragmatic results than with social theory. Even so, the Socialists made efforts to adjust to American practices and conditions, and the character of the party underwent changes.

In 1924 the Socialists had endorsed La Follette in the hope that a permanent third party would emerge. The hope quickly vanished as the American Federation of Labor regretted its support of the Conference for Progressive Political Action, and the conference itself could not agree to continue its third-party efforts. The Socialists withdrew from the CPPA. They had lost ground in the 1924 campaign. In 1926 Eugene V. Debs died, and the leadership passed, for a moment, into inept hands. For a few years the party did nothing more than concern itself with a few civil liberty cases, and the membership dwindled to less than 10,000.

Two things kept the Socialist Party from complete collapse. One was the depression, which seemed to furnish support for the Socialist analysis of the evils of capitalism, and the other was the rise of Norman Thomas to leadership. Thomas was a new type of Socialist leader. Whereas Debs had come into Socialism from the Labor movement, had little formal education, and addressed himself to the laboring man, Thomas came into Socialism from the Presbyterian ministry, held college degrees, had been an editor of a magazine, and secretary of the pacifist Fellowship of Reconciliation. In 1924, he was the Socialist candidate for Governor of New York. He was able to appeal to intellectuals, to Progressive reformers, and to non-Socialists.

With the help of the National Executive Committee, and of its executive secretary, Clarence Senior, Thomas rebuilt the Socialist Party. They established an efficient national office, and in 1928 Thomas ran for President.

The Socialists got on the ballot in 11 states, and polled 267,000 votes—a third of Debs' total eight years before. By 1932, with the help of the depression, the membership grew until it equalled that of 1908. It was, however, different in character. The new intellectuals contrasted strangely with the old guard who had supported Debs. Moreover, doctrinaire Marxists clashed with non-Marxist reformers in the party. That year Thomas campaigned against the depression, offering relief, reform, and recovery instead of orthodox Socialist assaults upon the capitalist system. The result was 882,000 votes—still less than Debs but clear promise that the party was out of the doldrums.

Franklin Roosevelt won the election of 1932, and the New Deal adopted many of the reformist panaceas which the Socialists had offered. At the same time, Adolf Hitler and his National Socialists came into power in Germany. In America, Thomas and the Socialists saw the New Deal was building state capitalism, had dangerous fascist tendencies, and failed to relieve suffering as fast as the Socialists wanted. In particular, the Socialists found the National Industrial Recovery Act and the Agricultural Adjustment Act bolstering capitalism and leading away from the Socialist commonwealth. Yet, many Socialists deserted the party to lend their aid to Roosevelt and the New Dealers.

In addition to losing talented men whom they could ill spare, the Socialists had bitter factional fights in their own ranks. In 1936, an "Old Guard" group, with strength in New York, Pennsylvania, and Connecticut, withdrew from the party and formed the Social Democratic Federation. Although it did not actively support Roosevelt, it withheld support from Thomas. That year, too, the needle trades defected to Roosevelt, while the "Trotskyite" Workers' Party dissolved itself and joined the Socialists. The accession brought more troubles than voters. In 1936, Thomas received 187,000 votes.

After 1936, the Socialist Party's decline was steady. In 1937 the party expelled the Trotskyites—who then formed the Socialist Workers' Party. The next year the Socialist vote in New York State was so small that it lost its place on the ballot. When war came in Europe in 1939, Thomas and the Socialists demanded absolute neutrality for the United States, but their isolationism brought no support.

In 1940, Thomas fell below 100,000 votes. Four years later, he had 80,000, though in 1948 he received 140,-000. In 1952, with a new candidate, Darlington Hoopes of Reading, Pennsylvania, the party's vote was down to 20,000.

The Communists. During the time that the Socialist Party was struggling to recover, the Communist Party, which had been formed in 1919, was achieving internal unity and developing a technique by which it could become effective. Originally formed from a split in the Socialist Party, the Communists spent the years until 1924 in factional fights, periodic expulsions of losing groups, and the effort to establish a workers' party. The factionalism was largely a conflict between a Russian-language federation and an English-speaking group which wanted to cooperate with left-wing Socialists. Neither had any very clear concept of Leninist doctrines, nor any tangible identification with American political traditions. If they lacked theory, however, they did not suffer from a scarcity of organizational leadership. Their leaders were good organizers who could discipline the few members, administer the affairs of the party, and manipulate a small, quick-moving group into an effective instrument for controlling larger and slower-moving political bodies. Yet, it was their failure to understand American politics that rendered them relatively impotent. The leaders believed, after the manner of Lenin, that the proper slogan, the clever maneuver, or the capacity to seize the psychological moment in a crisis would give them control of a great mass movement of the proletariat. They took their orders from the Comintern—which had no understanding of the American mind or the American laborer—and tried to achieve by "tactics" the ends which they might have achieved by good faith and fair appeal.

In its first two years the party split into two factions—the Communist Party and the United Communist Party. In May, 1921, under Moscow's orders, they united in the Communist Party of America. It's leader was William Z. Foster, a one-time Populist, a Bryan Democrat, and an active member of the I.W.W. (Industrial Workers of the World). He was a skillful organizer of labor unions. His talents kept the party from collapse under the attacks made by the government and internal dissensions. Governmental prosecution drove the party underground, but it reduced the membership to manageable proportions. The members were organized in cells, while the open and legal agency of the party was the Workers' Party.

In 1922 the Workers' Party, which had about 13,000 members, made campaigns in a few states. Its announced program was moderate, and it insisted that it was only supporting a labor party for America. Two years later Workers' Party men attended a convention of the Farmer Labor Party—which had withdrawn from the Conference for Progressive Political Action—and dominated the formation of the Federated Farmer Labor Party. The movement failed to deceive La Follette, who announced that he would not accept the endorsement of any group with Communist support. The Workers thereupon ran Foster for President and Benjamin Gitlow for Vice President under their own label. (*See Document No. 25.*)

For five more years factions disrupted the party. In 1925 Foster and his group appealed to Moscow against a faction headed by Charles Ruthenberg and Jay Lovestone —"the City College boys"—but an American Commission set up by the Comintern ordered that each group be equally represented on a new central-executive committee. In 1929 Foster won control when Lovestone backed Bukharin in his losing struggle with Stalin. Thereafter, the American party, shifting often to keep up with the changes in the Comintern's line, worked to build a strong organization. It abandoned the dream of creating a labor party, and asserted that the Communist Party was quickly becoming a mass-revolutionary party. Despite its efforts, the evidence was unconvincing. In 1928, Foster and Gitlow received 48,000 votes, in 1932 Foster and James Ford polled 103,000.

The Communists made every effort to capitalize on the depression. They organized Unemployed Councils, and promoted demonstration after demonstration of the jobless—but in time the workers, who wanted jobs rather than demonstrations, lost interest. More effective was the Communist work among Negroes. They seized upon the Scottsboro case and other outrages against Negroes to present themselves as the defenders of minority rights.

Their efforts contributed to making the party itself a tightly-organized, disciplined group which gave unquestioning obedience to the central committee.

About 1935, the party adopted a new and more successful policy. Franklin Roosevelt, facing a new recession, made a sharp turn to the left. Stalin, facing a growing fascism, moved toward a less violent attack on the capitalist democracies. In America the party announced it welcomed white-collar workers, and made overtures to the Socialists to unite in a Popular Front. The Socialists rejected the overtures, and the Communists moved on to bigger political game—the Democratic Party. It attacked Fascists, and won its first measure of acceptance and respectability. Soon its propaganda changed, and Communists appeared as patriots with Washington and Lincoln as progenitors of liberal movements. It created front organizations: the American League against War and Fascism won support of women and clergymen and intellectuals; the National Negro Congress spoke for the Communists among Negroes; the American Youth Movement, started by Liberals, fell under Communist control. More important, the party won power in the Congress of Industrial Organizations and controlled a number of labor unions. By 1940 the party had won power among intellectuals, and was spreading a new front—the American Peace Mobilization. When Hitler turned on Russia, however, the Communists became patriots and demanded war. With the war, the party membership rose rapidly, gaining recruits from government officers, editors, journalists and teachers. In an atmosphere of friendliness to Stalin, even business executives became Communists. Under Earl Browder, the party presented itself as the voice of Progressivism and the adherent of the principles of Scientific Socialism. By 1945 the party had 80,000 members.

But it had reached the peak of its influence. After the war, William Z. Foster regained control and the party repudiated the Browder doctrine that there were progressive tendencies in American capitalism. Instead, the party predicted depression and the economic collapse of America. It continued to misjudge the temper of the American labor movement—which was not revolutionary —and it offered the Negroes revolutionary violence instead of the acceptance in white American life which

Negro leaders desired. Moreover, as the cold war developed, the Communists supported Stalin at every juncture.

The party continued to promote front organizations. The International Workers Order offered insurance policies to 184,000 members. Schools of "Marxist studies," bearing the names of Jefferson and Lincoln, enrolled thousands of students. The Independent Citizens Committee of the Arts, Sciences, and Professions enlisted the support of actors from Broadway and Hollywood and of professional artists and writers.

But the policies of the party alienated some of its earlier supporters. Communists in the unions began to lose power as one union after another repudiated their leadership. Renewed attacks on religion drove ministers out of the party. The fervid adherence to Moscow cost the party support in government circles. The Committee of the Arts, Sciences, and Professions had been founded in 1944 to win support for Roosevelt's fourth term, and the National Citizens Political Action Committee had been a CIO agency for marshaling labor votes for Roosevelt. Late in December, 1946, the two groups united to form the Progressive Citizens of America—which was clearly determined to form a third party. The development led to the withdrawal of Liberals who were content with the Democratic Party. In the first week in January the alliance of the Liberal Democrats and the Communists in sundry front organizations came to an end. The Liberals formed the Americans for Democratic Action.

The People's Progressive Party. From its beginning, the Progressive Citizens of America, which accepted Communists as members and avowed its determination to form a third party, expected to nominate Henry A. Wallace for the presidency. In September, 1946, the Secretary of Commerce—who had been Vice President during Roosevelt's third term and might have been his successor had not Roosevelt discarded him for Harry Truman in 1944 —spoke to a joint meeting of the Committee of the Arts, Sciences, and Professions and the National Citizens Political Action Committee. Before going, Wallace showed his speech to President Harry Truman and received his approval. The speech contained the assertion that Great Britain's imperialism in the Near East would provoke Russia into declaring war. "I am neither anti-British nor pro-British—neither anti-Russian nor pro-Russian," he said. This, he added, was the policy of the Truman administration. "We must not let our Russian policy be guided or influenced by those inside or outside the United States who want war with Russia."

The speech brought immediate protest from Secretary of State James F. Byrnes who, in Paris, was standing firm against Russian demands. Byrnes told Truman that he was "shocked and angered" by Wallace's statements, and Truman agreed to silence Wallace for the duration of the Paris conference. But Truman permitted a letter, written by Wallace the previous July, to be published. The letter was even stronger than the speech. Byrnes was not satisfied with Truman's promise, and demanded that Wallace be dismissed. Truman complied and asked for Wallace's resignation.

Throughout the year following the formation of the Progressive Citizens of America the Communists worked to build a third party and to persuade Wallace to lead it. Wallace was not a Communist, but he was manipulated by them. Eventually, as it became evident that Truman would seek re-election, Wallace announced his Independent candidacy. Thereafter, Wallace moved closer to the Communists.

The announcement brought the Communist issue to a head. The American Labor Party of New York endorsed Wallace, and several right-wing Labor leaders resigned from the satellite party. In the CIO unions, a struggle between the Trumanites and the Communists brought almost the complete collapse of Communist influence in the unions. The PCA, however, rejoiced. In January, 1948, their convention in Chicago adopted resolutions denouncing the Marshall plan and the Truman Doctrine in foreign affairs, demanding that manufacture of atomic bombs be discontinued, promising public ownership of steel, coal, railroads and public utilities. It condemned red-baiting—a "Hitlerian technique" which had been "raised by the lords of finance as a smoke screen for the plots against democracy itself." Wallace appeared, blamed Big Business and Harry Truman for inflation, condemned monopoly, and pronounced both old parties united in a program leading to war. He and his followers were for peace.

The party received its formal christening in Philadelphia in July, 1948. (*See Document No. 26.*) The meeting showed clearly the Communist influence, and non-Communists began to drop away. At the beginning of the campaign political pundits predicted that Wallace would poll five million votes, sap Truman's strength, and throw the election to Republican Thomas Dewey. Yet, Wallace's strength fell away until the Progressive Party became nothing more than another Communist-front movement. The election was an upset, but Wallace was not a factor. To everyone's surprise, Truman defeated Dewey. To no one's surprise, Wallace won but one-and-a-half-million votes.

The defeat was more than a disaster for Henry A. Wallace. It marked the end of Communist influence in labor unions and in many liberal circles. The party clung to the Progressive organization for another four years, and in 1952 its nominee, Vincent Hallinan, got but 140,000 votes—64,000 of them from the American Labor Party of New York. Late in the 1940's and through the 1950's the party was isolated, and frequently persecuted. It was an agency of the Russian government and of international Communism,. The Korean War, the Smith Act making the party illegal, the exposure, trial, and execution of Communists as spies all worked against their regaining their former influence. In 1956 the American Labor Party officially disbanded. At the same time, the Negro supporters left the party. In 1956 Hungary and Poland cost more support. Within another year the publication of the *Daily Worker* ceased, and the party was clearly dead as a political force. It had never been really strong, though its rigid, totalitarian organization had given it unusual effectiveness. It had not been a part of the American tradition, and its analysis of American conditions, both economic and political, had been defective. Post-war prosperity, the cold war, and the defection of non-Communist leftists had combined to render it impotent.

The Dixiecrats. Perhaps the victory of Truman in the 1948 election carried a significance for all third-party movements in the future. The President won his re-election not only over Wallace, but over another third party which split away from the Democrats and threatened to destroy the party. The Dixiecrat revolt of the States'

Rights Democrats was both a more serious defection and a more important development than the Wallace movement.

Wallace, the Communists, and the liberals in the Democratic Party had alike grown impatient with Truman's failure to move rapidly toward the social program which he called the "Fair Deal." This involved expansion of social security, raising minimum wages, a fair-employment practices act, public housing, and slum clearance. Whereas the program appealed to liberals, Truman was unable to get his proposals through Congress. Moreover, he lost labor support when he invoked the sanctions of the Taft-Hartley Act in a railroad strike. The President's advisers told him that he needed to fear the Wallace movement and should move further to the left to combat it.

Hardly had the Chicago convention of the Progressives ended when Truman sent Congress a message about Civil Rights. He called for laws abolishing poll taxes, for making lynching, and segregation federal offenses. The proposals were designed to call back the departing liberals—instead it promptly drove the Southern Bourbons to desperation. The Southern Governors' conference in Florida issued a reply to Truman asserting that unless the administration ceased its assaults on white supremacy, the Southerners would revolt. They talked of a Southern Democratic Party, of reviving the two-thirds rule in Democratic Conventions. When the Truman forces carried the Democratic convention and wrote a civil-rights plank in the platform, the delegates from Alabama and Mississippi withdrew from the convention. In a few days, joined by other states, they organized the States' Rights Democratic Party, denounced the civil rights proposals of the Northern Democrats, and nominated Governor J. Strom Thurmond of South Carolina for President and Mississippi's Governor Fielding Wright for Vice President.

The Dixiecrats were not alone concerned with civil rights and Negro equality. They were opposed to the entire leftist program of the Democrats. They deplored the "gradual but certain growth of a totalitarian state" and were opposed to "centralized, bureaucratic government and the police state." Wealthy natural-gas and oil promoters in the Southwest objected to federal regulation, private utility interests opposed the competition of the Tennessee Valley Authority. Southern states condemned the Supreme Court's decision that oil wells located on the continental shelf under the Gulf of Mexico were under the control of the federal government.

The States' Rights Democrats had no hope of electing Thurmond and Wright. They hoped, however, to prove to the Democratic Party that it needed the votes of the South by throwing the election into the House of Representatives. The attempt failed. Wallace failed to draw enough leftist votes from the Democrats to make the Rightist vote significant. Thurmond polled 1,169,000 votes and carried South Carolina, Alabama, Mississippi, and Louisiana—and received the vote of one Tennessee elector for a total of 39 electoral votes. Despite both Wallace and Thurmond—and Dewey—Truman won with a plurality of 114 electoral votes. In the popular vote he had 180,000 less than his combined opponents.

Although the States' Rights Democrats ran a separate electoral ticket, they proclaimed that they were not a third party. "This is not a bolt," said Governor Fielding Wright. "This is not a fourth party. I say to you that we are the true Democrats of the Southland and these United States." In a sense, he was defining what had become a new political phenomenon in the United States—the organized party within a party, or a satellite party. These were something more than pressure groups, something less than full-fledged parties waging an independent campaign.

The experience of third parties in the twentieth century had shown that without local organizations—in counties, cities and states—a national third party could not hope to win. The Socialists and the Communists had demonstrated that trade unions, or even local societies—"cells" —could not take the place of local political machines and a working group of local office-holders and candidates. The Bull Moose and the La Follette Progressives had both failed to build a solid base at the "grass roots," and the Wallace Progressives were giving a new illustration of the fact that a successful party needed more than a national program and a zealous candidate for the presidency. It needed candidates for sheriffs, aldermen, county boards, state legislatures, and Congress. Experience had shown, too, that third parties had to overcome legal obstacles in getting a place on the ballots. Although it was true that in states having a majority of the electoral college, getting on the ballot was hardly more than a formality, the states with large populations required a large number of signatures on petitions and nominating papers. Here, too, strong local organizations of interested office-seekers might serve a useful role.

In the 'thirties, two other third-party efforts had illustrated the difficulties before those who would launch an independent campaign. In 1936, a coalition of Father Charles Coughlin's "Social Justice" followers, who advocated silver inflation and the nationalization of banks, utilities, and natural resources, combined with the remnants of Senator Huey Long's "Share the Wealth" movement— now led by Gerald K. Smith—to form the Union Party and nominate William Lemke, Non-Partisan League Congressman from North Dakota, for the presidency. Lemke polled almost 900,000 votes. Two years later, Phillip F. La Follette, who had served three terms as Governor of Wisconsin, called on all liberal opponents of Roosevelt to unite in a National Progressive Party. The liberals did not respond. Instead, Rooseveltians, Socialists, and Communists shouted in unison that the voter's cross in a circle which served as a party emblem was a Nazi swastika. The movement gained no supporters.

Satellite Parties. Instead of rallying to a third-party movement, the Liberals preferred to work through satellite parties. Early examples of the satellite party, exercising local power while still revolving in the orbit of a national party were the Non-Partisan League of the Dakotas, the Progressive Party of Wisconsin, and the Farmer-Labor Party of Minnesota. The first maintained a high degree of independence from its origins in 1916 until the New Deal—and then, though endorsing Roosevelt, sent critical representatives to Congress. The Progressive Party of Wisconsin grew out of the La Follette Progressive faction in the Republican Party. For a decade in the 'thirties and 'forties it maintained an independent existence in the state, and eventually returned to the Republican ranks. The Farmer-Labor Party actually ran its own presidential candidate, Parley P. Christensen of Utah, in 1920, and succeeded for a time in maintaining a balance between farmers and laborers. They split, however, and the farmers went back into the Republican Party while the remnants dominated by Communist CIO unions, entered a coalition with the Democrats.

In the 1930's New York unions and the Social Democratic Federation which had split from the Socialists, formed the American Labor Party for the thinly veiled purpose of keeping Roosevelt from swinging too far to the right. It supported Roosevelt, but perhaps its greatest significance was that it made easier the Communist infiltration into the Democratic Party. As the ALP became increasingly a fellow-traveling vehicle, Social Democrats and non-Communist liberals withdrew to form another satellite party—the Liberal Party—which continued to revolve in Roosevelt's orbit. When the American Labor Party supported Wallace and the third party Progressives, it collapsed. Each of these parties, while they existed, served to exert pressure on the candidates and the office-holders of the major parties, helped create the "grass roots" strength which the major parties needed, and gave their supporters a means of expressing a degree of dissent from the major party's policies. They elected local officials and Congressmen who could exert an influence on the manner of administration and on legislation. Perhaps the satellite party, working on and through the major party, could perform much of the role which third parties had had in American history.

Conclusion. For a dozen years, and three more presidential elections after the States' Rights revolt and the Wallace Progressives, there was little talk in the United States of third parties. Vegetarians, Greenbackers, Prohibitionists, and sundry representatives of the extreme left continued to run insignificant campaigns but the voters ignored them to choose between Dwight Eisenhower and Adlai Stevenson or John Kennedy and Richard Nixon. Factions continued in both the Democratic and Republican ranks, and Liberals and Conservatives in each gave enthusiastic support to favored leaders. The national conventions were colorful, televised spectacles, but after the delegates had chosen their nominees, the party faithful closed ranks to present their unified, and often indistinguishable faces, to the "enemy." No specter of a third party frightened the supporters of either the Democrats or the Republicans.

Yet, no political leader could afford to remain unaware of the role that third parties had played in the history of American politics. Occasionally, lesser parties had produced leaders—Thurlow Weed, Thaddeus Stevens, Charles Sumner, for example—for later major parties. More often, the third parties had offered opportunities to discontented leaders of the major parties who carried their followers into revolt and brought disaster to their former associates. Three third parties had been headed by ex-Presidents, and if Millard Fillmore's Know-Nothings of 1856 could not be given complete credit for James Buchanan's victory over John C. Frémont, certainly Martin Van Buren took enough votes from Lewis Cass to elect Zachary Taylor in 1848, and Theodore Roosevelt's Bull Moose Progressives in 1912 defeated Taft and elected Wilson. Two Vice Presidents—John C. Breckinridge in 1860 and Henry Wallace in 1948—headed third-party movements. Most of the leaders whom the major parties furnished to the minor ones were soreheads seeking for revenge, but the experience suggested that party politicians might well pause before giving offense to their one-time leaders.

Perhaps the major role that third parties had played had been that of promoting new governmental ideas and programs. Many reforms which were first offered by third parties were, in time and after they had received wide popular approval, accepted and put into operation by the major parties. Then, too, many ideas which third parties, at one time or another, put forward failed to be well received and were forgotten. The third parties served as pilot plants for testing new ideas.

But most of all the third parties of American history— the various shades of Progressives, the many manifestations of labor's penchant for political experimenting, the Liberty, and Free Soil, and Anti-Masonic Parties—had served to strengthen the two-party system. Essentially, each of the two parties represented great conglomerates of different interests, different ideas, and different purposes. The leaders and program makers of each party arranged and executed compromises between the different opinions and the diverse programs. It was through the compromises, the conciliations, the adjustments that the United States stayed united. Essentially, it was a government by unanimity—and in their curious way the third parties contributed to the political and governmental harmony which brought success to the American democratic system.

Part II
DOCUMENTS

AN ANTIMASON ANALYZES
HIS PARTY, 1827-1828[1]

Frederick Whittlesey, a member of the New York Anti-masonic party's central committee, wrote an account of the beginnings of the party for Jabez Hammond, who was collecting material for a political history of New York State. In this selection Whittlesey indicates how the emotional fervor aroused by Antimasonry tapped new sources of political activity, and discusses the party's impact on the political structure of New York.

✦   ✦   ✦

It is not necessary here, nor does it come within the scope of this treatise at all, to say whether the views of the anti-masons were right or wrong; whether their principle of exclusion of free masons was worthy or unworthy of themselves or the country; whether their manner of political action was justifiable or prudent or otherwise; those topics may find an appropriate place in a treatise of another character. In order to show fairly the causes of the rise of the anti-masonic party, as a political party, it has been deemed necessary to say thus much of its origin, as its rise is intimately connected with the outrage upon Morgan; but the history of that transaction, important though it may be in another point of view, will only be adverted to here as connected with the rise and progress of the political party whose history is now under consideration.

Though this was the starting point of anti-masonry as a political party, yet it is not to be understood that this party even then, or until some considerable time afterwards, assumed the perfect form and feature of an or-

---

[1] Jabez D. Hammond, *The History of Political Parties in the State of New York* (2 vols, Syracuse, New York, 1852), II:379-392.

ganized party. The town elections . . . were the results of the desultory and spontaneous efforts of the people themselves in different towns. Those who were generally considered as political leaders were mostly averse to taking political ground in this manner. Their old party ties and associations were still cherished; and practised politicians upon either side were averse to abandoning the parties with which they had so long acted. Some of them desired to preserve and continue the old party organization, but so to conduct their respective operations as to prevent the nomination of masons by the conventions of either political party. In this way it was hoped by some, that masonry could be effectually put down in a quiet manner, without incurring the imputation of removing old political landmarks, or dissolving old political associations. If reflection did not, subsequent circumstances did show, that all such speculations were idle. Masons were no more willing to be proscribed in the conventions than at the polls, and it might have been foreseen that one party or the other would bid for their aid. The then posture of political parties, both in regard to state and national politics, may, and probably did, have something to do in making anti-masonry political. Mr. Clinton had been elected governor, and it began by this time to be understood that he would unite with Mr. Van Buren in the support of Gen. Jackson for the presidency. This determination of Mr. Clinton was not acceptable to many of his political friends. On the other hand, a large portion of the bucktails at the west were dissatisfied with the former movement of their political friends to force the nomination of Mr. Crawford; they were suspicious that the recent election of Mr. Clinton was produced by the supineness if not the treachery of their political friends at the east, and they were jealous of the reputed union between Mr. Clinton and Mr. Van Buren to secure the vote of the state for Gen. Jackson. All these circumstances gave the politicians of the Clintonian party, opposed to General Jackson, who were upon the committees of investigation, a convenient opportunity, by operating upon the prevalent public sentiment against masonry, to direct the attention of those who were thus hostile to masonry, to the fact that both Gov. Clinton and General Jackson were high masons, and that their political union was another evidence of masonic influence; and thus stimulate this sentiment to the opposition of both. . . . As the situation of political parties at that time furnished shrewd and calculating politicians with opportunities for so directing the prevalent public feeling, it has been supposed that they took advantage of it to give such direction to public action. Possibly something of this kind may have been done or attempted; yet a careful consideration of the state of public sentiment at that time must satisfy any one that but little could have been effected in this way. In a state of high excitement in any community few can remain cool and unaffected by the prevalent public sentiment; and those that do, by not entering into the feeling themselves, have seldom the power of giving direction to public feeling. . . .

The truth is, the public were highly excited, and the excitement pervaded all classes of people. If the more practised politicians were desirous of giving a different direction to the public feeling, they found it was substantially out of their power. The people had themselves determined to bring the subject of free masonry to the test of the ballot box, laying out of view all other political questions, and those who felt with them were constrained to follow the popular impulse. The investigation of the abduction during the summer of 1827, had made many converts to this sentiment, and before the fall elections came on, those who were determined to make masonry a test at the elections, were a majority in several counties, though the fact was not generally believed until after the elections were held. During all this time, and indeed during the whole contest, the masons complained of this course as unjust and proscriptive. And on the other hand the Anti-masons, even while preparing their tickets for the canvass, strenuously insisted that their objects were not political. They seemed at first to have had an earnest desire to escape the imputation of making anti-masonry a political party. . . . They only committed themselves not to support a mason of any party; and as neither political party would adopt that rule of exclusion, they were forced to run a ticket of their own; but by so doing, they did not mean to consider themselves bound to support the measures of either political party. They had an object of their own to accomplish, which was of paramount importance in their estimation, and they asked all citizens of whatever former politics, to aid them in the accomplishment of this object. By this general invitation they would offend the previous political feelings or prejudices of none. If this invitation was accepted by the mass of voters, the former political parties would be broken up and destroyed. This result was of course foreseen by the politicians of all parties. The political leaders were, however, desirous of preserving the organization of the respective parties. Many of them were not sufficiently imbued with the spirit of hostility to the masons to take ground with the new party; many of them thought the basis of the anti-masonic party was too narrow and proscriptive to meet with success; or, if it was successful, that the ascendancy would be temporary and ephemeral; and so they determined to stand by their old party discipline and usages. This was rather the feeling previous to the election of 1827. The bucktails made their nominations—the Adams party made theirs—and the anti-masons made theirs without any regard to previous political distinctions. The result astonished all—even the anti-masons themselves—and opened the eyes of politicians to the growing power of this new party. At this election, the anti-masons carried Genesee, Monroe, Livingston, Orleans and Niagara counties, in face of both the other parties.

At this election, the candidates of the Adams party received but few votes comparatively. . . . The Adams party was left with but few in numbers: composed mostly of Clintonians, who, though masons, were unwilling to join the Jackson party and could not act with the anti-masons, and some Clintonians who were not masons, and were unwilling to act with either of the other parties. The anti-masonic party was composed of a large majority of the old Clintonian party . . . and a very considerable portion of the bucktail party, comprising a great force in votes at the polls, and, perhaps, not a great force of the old political leaders. It is to be observed, that these remarks are to be deemed to be confined to the western counties, commonly called 'the infected district,' where anti-masonry had its origin.

A new party thus organized, like the anti-masonic party, of materials never before accustomed to be assimilated, comparatively without leaders, and having but one object in view, and moved by a feeling of high excitement, would not be likely to be choice in the selection of their candidates. . . .

During this time there were many secessions from the masonic fraternity, and the seceding members not only confirmed the truth of Morgan's "Illustrations" of the first degree of masonry, but penetrated farther into the arcana of the masonic mysteries, and disclosed the ceremonies and obligations of several of the higher degrees of masonry. These disclosures induced the anti-masons to receive the seceding members into their fellowship, and welcome them with warmth into their ranks, with every assurance of protection. They contributed also to still further excite the public feeling in the western counties against the institution, and to prompt them to greater exertions to abolish it through the medium of the ballot box. The institution was now looked upon as based on principles dangerous in a free government, subversive of political equality, and hostile to the impartial administration of justice. The overthrow of the institution was now the principal object to be accomplished, and the abduction of Morgan was referred to as one among the many evidences of the dangerous and secret power of free masonry. Converts to the side of anti-masonry increased rapidly. In March, 1828, the first general convention was held at Le Roy upon this subject, and was composed of delegates from twelve of the western counties. The delegates were numerous and highly respectable for their standing and character. The whole scope of the proceedings of this convention was to present to the public the dangerous principles of free masonry, to excite attention to it, and evoke action against it. This, as at the first, was the only point to which action was asked. There was no political resolution passed, except that which declared that free masonry was unworthy to exist in a free government. Yet this convention was political in its object in this sense, that it endeavored to bring public opinion to bear upon the institution of free masonry through the ballot box. . . .

Although the anti-masons claimed to stand independent of both political parties; and although, as a party, they had neither avowed nor expressed any opinion upon the great and leading measures of the country, yet it soon became quite evident that this party must eventually be forced into opposition to the Jackson party. Gen. Jackson himself was a high mason, and could not, upon the fundamental principles of anti-masonry, in any event, be supported by them. The anti-masons required a civil proscription of masons. The Jackson party in the state could not yield to this requirement without breaking up the bonds of their strength and perilling its power; and the anti-masonic members of the state legislature generally went with the national republicans as to measures. All these circumstances clearly indicated that the anti-masonic party must eventually be forced into opposition to the Jackson party.

— Document No. 2 —

THE DEMISE OF THE ANTIMASONIC PARTY, 1833 [2]

In 1830 William H. Seward, later to become Secretary of State under Abraham Lincoln, began his long political career by winning election as an Antimason to the New York State Senate. Seward was typical of the many men with political aspirations who achieved their first successes as Antimasons, and who later moved into the newly-formed Whig party as the political opposition to Masonry waned. Here Seward discusses the decline of Antimasonry and his abandonment of the movement.

After this disastrous defeat [*in the 1833 elections*] not a particle of hope remained that the Antimasonic party could successfully challenge the political power of the country. We were obliged to admit that, in the two chief objects of its organization, it had failed. Its first object

---

[2] Frederick W. Seward, editor, *William H. Seward: An Autobiography* (New York, 1891), pp. 147-148.

was to restore the supremacy of the laws of the State, by bringing to the judgment and punishment which those laws denounced the conspirators and murderers of William Morgan. With a larger experience since that time, I have become satisfied that no political movement, however successful otherwise, succeeds in accomplishing an object so simple and so definite as this. For a long time I agreed with those who thought that the late civil war would fail of one of its chief ends, if it should fail to convict Jefferson Davis, or other distinguished rebels, in a court of justice. The second object of the Antimasonic party was, the establishment of the principle that popular secret combinations, with oaths and penalties, capable of being directed to act politically, judicially, or socially but secretly, ought to be condemned and made odious. This object also failed, while it seemed to triumph. If it was mortifying, a few years afterward, to see the institution of freemasonry reappear, in its ancient life and vigor, after having been left for dead on the field of combat, it was some consolation to see that, if the warnings of the Antimasonic party against secret political combinations had been accepted by the people, the country would have been spared the shame of the pitiful 'Know-nothing' conspiracy, and the dangerous order of the 'Golden Circle' which claimed to inaugurate the late rebellion. However we might think on this subject, it was now apparent that our occasion had passed by, and that to continue to flaunt the Antimasonic banner, when not a single recruit was to be gained, and no past defeat could be retrieved, would be to sink that noble and patriotic organization into a mere discontented, litigious, retaliatory faction. These reflections brought us to a unanimous agreement that, so far as might depend on our action, the Antimasonic party should be dissolved, and every member of it left at liberty to act as his judgment and conscience should dictate, without censure or complaint from his former associates.

After reaching this conclusion, some naturally asked the others what use we should make of our new liberty. I answered, for myself: "While I see no present organization for combined action except the Democratic party, I see too much in the policy and principles of that party to think of giving it my adhesion. I have opposed it from its beginning, throughout its aggressive career, and in its public triumph, as entertaining principles and policy injurious to the public welfare, subversive of the Constitution, and dangerous to public liberty. If I shall prove wrong in this, I shall have no longer occasion nor justification for political activity. If I am right in these opinions, time will show it, and necessity will bring round the associations with which I can labor for the welfare, safety, and advancement, of the country."

These opinions were accepted generally by my old political associates. A few, however, with more or less directness, availed themselves of their new freedom to join the triumphant Democratic party under General Jackson.

— Document No. 3 —

ANALYSIS OF WORKINGMEN'S PARTY, 1830[3]

Factionalism developed early in the short history of the New York City Workingmen's Party and proved to be an important factor in the Party's rapid disintegration. Less than a year after the Party's organization, it had split into three separate groups: The major Noah Cook-Anti-State Guardianship faction, the Robert Dale Owen-State Guardianship faction, and the small Thomas Skidmore Agrarian faction. In the following article, an Owen-faction editor explains the purposes and differences of these three groups and makes some scathing comments on the Democratic Party of New York.

✓   ✓   ✓

Parties in New York. The following appears in a late number of the *National Intelligencer.*

[3] *New York Sentinel and Working Man's Advocate,* July 28, 1830.

"To all persons within the bounds of the state, the parties and politics of New York are as puzzling as were the enigmas of the ancient Sphinx. After some fifteen years study, people abroad had begun to get some insight into the mystery of party denominations there; when, on a sudden, a year or so ago, a host of new sects sprung up, almost swallowing the old, and, like the shaking of a kaleidoscope, presenting an aspect totally different, though composed of materials identically the same. This sudden change was enough to puzzle the great magician himself; (and one object of his present visit may be for aught we know, to study the new state of things, and ascertain how the elements of old parties have combined in forming the new—this, however, by the way.) For our own parts, if any body this side of Communipaw can tell what are the distinguishing principles, objects, characters, or affinities of the Agrarians—the Workies—the Regulars—the Regency—the Infidels, so called—the Mechanic Working—the Wrightsmen—the Radicals—the Skeletons —not to mention the more familiar Tammanies, Bucktails, &c., &c., it is more than we can do, and we fairly 'give it up.' In fact, on this subject, we find ourselves in the predicament of certain worthy members of Congress, who, when a question is put which they do not understand, or have not attended to, look round to see whether others, in whom they have confidence, rise or sit."

We doubt not, New York politics are puzzling enough to strangers. Even our own citizens—so industrious have intriguing politicians been in casting dust in their eyes— find it no easy matter to solve the modern political riddles of our city.

We happen to have been eye-witnesses of the last year's affray since its very commencement; and having during that time had no interests to serve, except when we believed to be "the greatest good of the greatest number," if the *Intelligencer* will receive at our hands a plain statement of facts, it is at his service.

He needs not to be informed who the Tammany-men, Regulars, Regency, or by whatever name friends or foes designate them, are. If a name can give a character, they are "Democratic Republicans." If deeds not words are to be the test, they are the party in office, enjoying what they have got, and casting about to see how they shall keep it and get more; fattening on the loaves and fishes, and becoming lazy and saucy in proportion as they get fat. They are the political descendants of those men who, thirty years ago, rallied at the cry of "Jefferson and Democracy!" who supported the patriot-statesman through good and through bad report, and gave to this republic, in the person on him whom the rich and the proud denounce as a leveller and an infidel, a Chief Magistrate such as we may never see again: but if you seek in modern Tammany the likeness of their political fathers, you will lose your time and your pains. Throughout the country, indeed, you will still find attached to the party, a remnant of the original stock—but look to the regular leaders—the mill-horse nomination men—and you will find them just what all *mere* political men are—scramblers for office, and men who talk of public good as a bore, or a chimera.

To the corruptions of this once democratic and now venal party, the so-called "Working Men's party" owes its origin. We were tired of hearing empty professions yearly repeated—tired of seeing political harpies make sale of public offices—tired of having the shadow for the reality, and of witnessing the interests of the industrious many, shamelessly sacrificed for the exalting and false advantaging of the indolent few. We longed to see a "Nation party"—a party that should embrace the honest of all political sects—that should bear for its motto "Principles not men," and act up to the motto it bore. Universal and Equal Education is the first great object for which the "Working Men's party" contends. We see in Equal Education the only effective and peaceful means to secure the exercise of equal rights and the chance of equal enjoyment to every citizen of the republic; and we perceive that freedom and equality are, to the mass of the people, but empty sounds, until both are planted there, where alone they can grow, in the human mind.

For the nicknames which our enemies have chosen to attach to us—Agrarians, Workies, Wrightsmen, Radicals, Levellers, and half a dozen more—they are but the second edition of those that were put forth in 1801 to cheat the people into the belief that those who spoke of Liberty and Equality meant Atheistical Persecution and Licentiousness.

There *is,* however, an Agrarian party in this city—a very small one, but still a party; who tell us very honestly that they wish to see a general "rupping up," (as they call it) to have all the property of the State sold at a National Auction, and an equal portion dealt out to every man and woman.

These are—and call themselves—Agrarians; by which term is now understood in this city, those who desire an equal division of property among all adults. Their organ is the "Friend of Equal Rights," edited by Messrs. Ming & Skidmore; and they are very bitter against all who will not swallow their political creed entire, without scruple or hesitation—especially against the "Education men," as they commonly call us.

One other party—or rather hodge-podge of parties—still remains to be spoken of. It is easier to say what *it is not* than what it *is.* It is *not* the Tammany party and *not* the Working Men's party; and *every thing except these* (if we may judge by the late Ward election) it is. Its leaders compose about as motley a group as might be found in the political ranks, from Maine to Missouri. The "Working Men" was a popular name; so they got hold of it; and have contrived, by its help, and by dint of great professions of horror for infidelity and agrarianism, to tack together, for the moment, the patchwork of a party, in which Stone of the *Commercial,* Charles King of the *American,* Dwight of the *Daily Advertiser,* Arthur Tappan of Church and State notoriety, and all their aiders and abettors, figure by the side of a few honest mechanics (too easy-tempered and short sighted to suspect the cheat) as the real, genuine "Working Men" of the City of New York!

And so ends our catalogue. We do not think the *Intelligencer* will obtain a more honest or correct one.

— Document No. 4 —

THE FLOUR RIOT, FEBRUARY 13, 1837[4]

Succumbing as a party in 1832, New York Working-men re-entered politics in 1834 at the height of the Bank War and became Jacksonian Democrats. Unable to subdue the "monopoly" faction of the Democracy, the Working-men formed the Equal Rights—or Loco Foco—Party in 1835. A third force in New York City politics but unable to build more than a weak State organization, the Loco Focos advocated equal rights for everyone and proclaimed their hostility to all monopolies, paper money, and "vested rights" by legislation. The men, measures, and name of the Party gradually were absorbed by a "purified" Tammany and the Democratic Party. In his history of the Party, Fitzwilliam Byrdsall, its Recording Secretary, described the relation of a Loco Foco rally to the New York "flour riot," an episode in the Party's brief, but stormy, career.

✓   ✓   ✓

About the beginning of February, the high prices of the necessaries of life were severely felt by the working population of this city, and discontent was extensively prevailing, especially towards the flour dealers; and the Loco Focos were up against Bank Monopolies, which afforded facilities to speculators. . . .

Ever vigilant in its opposition to all monopolies, the Equal Rights Party seized the present occasion as favorable to its constant object, to overcome its enemy. With this view, and to strengthen itself in public opinion, a

[4] Fitzwilliam, Byrdsall, *The History of the Loco-Foco or Equal Rights Party* (New York, 1842), pp. 99-105.

meeting was called in the Park by large bills posted throughout the city, as follows:

BREAD, MEAT, RENT, AND FUEL!
Their prices must come down!

The VOICE of THE PEOPLE shall be heard and will prevail! The people will meet in the Park, rain or shine, at 4 o'clock, p.m., on Monday afternoon, to inquire into the cause of the present unexampled distress and to devise a suitable remedy. All friends of humanity determined to resist monopolists and extortioners are invited to attend.

MOSES JAQUES	WARDEN HAYWARD
PAULUS HEDL	DANIEL GORHAM
DANIEL A. ROBERTSON	JOHN WINDT

ALEXANDER MING, JR.

The afternoon of the 13th, February, 1837, was intensely cold and extremely windy, and yet the meeting in the Park presented a dense multitude of many thousands. The venerable Moses Jaques was chosen Chairman, and there was he, who had seen over sixty winters, standing on a platform the most exposed to the inclemency of the blast, his countenance expressive of that righteous benevolence, which told us plainly as the hand of God could write it on the face of man, that his heart was with the people, devoted to the cause of humanity. Alexander Ming, Jr., ever one of the foremost in the same cause, addressed the people with his usual fearlessness of consequences to himself. He told them that the resolutions in his hand traced the present state of things to the right cause, "Our monstrous banking system." That the banks were the oppressors of the poor, for they fostered speculations in real estate, which raised rents, and they afforded facilities to forestalling of provisions, which raised the prices of the necessaries of life. But he exhorted his fellow citizens to seek peaceful remedies for public grievances, "To do no act which might bring into dispute the fair fame of a New Yorker, the honor of a citizen of this Republic, or the character of man." He then proceeded to read the following preamble, and a series of resolutions. . . .

These proceedings had scarcely been approved of by

the assemblage, when a stream of population, which had come down Chatham street, entered the Park, and then a man mounted the platform and addressed the multitude. His speech was directed against the flour dealers, and he added "go to the flour stores and offer a fair price, and if refused, take the flour." No sooner had he uttered those words, than the president of the meeting, Mr. Jaques, interposed promptly, and with the assistance of the officers of the meeting pulled him off the stand. The meeting then peaceably adjourned. But according to Mayor Clark's statement some one cried out "Hart's flour store"; and said a neutral paper of that period, "a body of nearly one thousand persons separated from the general mass, and proceeded to Washington street, and commenced an attack upon the store of Eli Hart and Co., the well known flour merchants of 173 & 175 of that street, completely filled the floor to the ceiling, from the basement to the roof, from the front to the rear, with barrels of flour and bags of wheat."

"The store was soon entered," Mayor Clark states, "barrels of flour thrown out and dashed to pieces in Washington street. Mayor Lawrence with a few officers repaired thither, but he and they were driven away. In a short time the mob had undisputed possession of that vast storehouse. Many of Mr. Hart's books and papers were seized, torn and scattered along the public streets. One of the Journals of that day stated that Mr. Hart's loss was about 500 barrels of flour and 1,000 bushels of wheat. This is probably a high estimate."

There were depredations committed on the same night on other flour stores in the city. Fifty-three of the rioters were apprehended by the police.

A portion of the city press would not let such a chance escape of attaching infamy to the Loco-Focos. Alexander Ming was falsely charged with having uttered the words, "go to the flour stores and offer a fair price for flour, and if refused, take the flour." The portion of the city press alluded to, is that which is subsidized by the advertising and other patronage of the monopoly and commercial aristocracy. Such a mercenary press, ever anxious to show its vassalage to the interests of its lords, is always up, and more eager to oppose reform and reformers than its masters are themselves. Hence those venal presses were only laboring in their vocation when they slandered and reviled the Loco-Focos, who were reformers contending for just principles, and not flour rioters.

But it afterwards came out, as stated by the Journal of Commerce, which sometimes gives sudden emissions of conscientious acknowledgments, that "a letter was found in the Park some days before the meeting took place, addressed to Mr. H. Lennox by an anonymous person, informing him that the store of Hart & Co. was to be plundered one of these nights by a large party of men, and that in order to enable them to carry their design into execution, two alarms of fire were to be given, one near the Battery, and the other higher up the city, and whilst the watchmen and police were assembled at these two points, the conspirators were to break open the store and carry off the flour. The letter was brought to High Constable Hays, who showed it to Hart & Co. Besides this, other anonymous letters of a similar import came to the Mayor, who caused the contents to be made known to Hart & Co."

Of the fifty-three rioters arrested by the public authorities, *not one* was a Loco-Foco. Had there been even one, it would have gone forth from the city press to the whole Union as proof against the whole party. Besides, the latter appointed a committee to examine the rolls of names of the members of the party, with the view of expelling any guilty member, and not one was found. How could men who were strenuously contending for Rights, be the perpetrators of wrongs? Above all these facts, the whole history of the party was proof, that it was against monopolies by legislation, and especially banks, that the Equal Rights Democracy were contending; and the last resolution passed at the Park meeting was *"that the true remedy for the people, which will reduce the price of all the necessaries of life is, that every working man refuse paper money in payment for his services, or demand specie at the banks for all notes paid to him. . . .*

— Document No. 5 —

THE ANTIRENT STATE CONVENTION, BERNE, NEW YORK, JANUARY 15, 1845 [5]

In 1844 Van Rensselaer tenants made a concerted effort to influence elections to the New York Assembly. Encouraged by the success of their venture into politics, the Antirenters held their first state convention early in 1845. At the meeting the delegates passed resolutions deprecating the use of violence against the landlords, decided to approve a slate of Antirent candidates for the coming elections, and drew up a petition to the legislature asking for redress of specific grievances.

✓   ✓   ✓

WHEREAS—The time has arrived when it becomes necessary for us, as citizens and tenants, residing on manors, claimed and leased by landlords under grants from foreign Governments, thus in a formal and public manner to correct false representations and misapplied constructions of the designs and purposes of the Antirent Associations in the various counties in this state. Public functionaries, and also the press, both powerful organs, have widely spread charges of combination of tenants for the secret purpose of hiring persons disguised as Indians, to set law at defiance, and obtaining right by might. When the public mind is abused, it is calculated to defeat the objects sought for, and tends to bring associations into disrepute—therefore we publicly declare—before God and man—that no such combinations have been made within our knowledge or belief, and can exist in imagination. The associations of tenants are for honorable and legal redress of grievances, to be obtained from

[5] *The Albany Argus,* February 11, 1845.

the proper tribunals. The only services employed are legal counsels—the only expenses, those for publications, the attendance on courts and sessions of the Legislature. Over the acts of individuals the associations have no control, and therefore disclaim any accountability. . . .

RESOLVED, That in the opinion of this Convention the late and lamentable scenes in the county of Rensselaer in which sacrifice of human life occurred, present a case, which calls loudly for the censure of a civilized and enlightened community against all and every act infringing in the least upon law and order, and that we entirely disavow all and any connection with lawless and reckless desperadoes. . . .

RESOLVED, That we will discard and discountenance any man or men pretending to be our friend who grasp at any adverse report, and who countenance, exaggerate and circulate such as truths, to the detriment of our individual and party rights.

RESOLVED, That we will adhere to our heretofore expressed opinion through the ballot boxes, and sustain nominations made as *Anti-rent*, laying aside all old party lines, either Whig or Democratic, and in nominating our candidates, we will endeavor to select men who have been with us in our days of adversity as well as prosperity, who are and have been Anti-rent men at all times.

RESOLVED, That we deeply regret that the Governor of this State should "feel himself precluded from inviting the careful attention of the legislature to the consideration" of the acknowledged grievances of the tenants, by reason of the lawless and indefensible acts of a misguided few, with whose acts and doings he truly expresses his conviction that the great body of the "tenant farmers" are in no wise connected, and which they totally discountenance—but we cannot but deprecate this act of injustice, in making the sins of others the ground of withholding all relief from the acknowledged burden of oppression resting upon us.

RESOLVED, That we cannot conceive of any sufficient cause for the continuance of "contracts" which are acknowledged to be "onerous in their exactions, and tenures which in their nature and character are uncongenial with the habits and opinions of a free people," and the principles of a free government.

RESOLVED, That we fully and heartily concur in the sentiment of our State Executive, that the "theory upon which our government is instituted, is equal protection to all." Yet while we make this concession we most deeply deplore that the practical effect of our laws relating to landlord and tenant is diametrically opposed to such theory. . . .

The committee on petitions was then announced, and through Mr. Thompson, chairman of the committee, reported the following, which was unanimously adopted:—

To the Hon. The Legislature of the State of New York. —The undersigned, legal voters and citizens of the county of —— conceiving the existing laws of this state relating to Landlord and Tenant to be unjust, oppressive, and diametrically opposed to the spirit of free and Republican institutions, do hereby petition your Honorable body for the passage of an act repealing all laws granting special privileges to Landlords in the collection of their rents, so that they shall be permitted to use and enjoy the common right of other creditors, in the collection of their dues, and none other.

And the undersigned do further petition your Honorable body for the passage of an act authorizing tenants, when prosecuted for rents, to set up as a defense against such prosecution, the want of a good and sufficient title to the premises in the landlord or prosecutor; and that such defense be a bar to any recovery against such tenant until the title of the landlord be fully established; to apply in those cases where lands have been leased for a long series of years or in perpetuity.

And your petitioners do further ask for the passage of a law authorizing and directing the Assessors of the several towns of this State to estimate and consider the amount of rents charged on lease-hold premises, leased for a term of fifteen years and upwards, situated in their respective towns, as the interest of a principle, which principle shall be assessed to the owners of such premises and the taxes thereon to be paid in the towns within which such lands are situated, for their benefit, and in case of default of payment of such taxes, that such leasehold premises be returned in like manner as non-resident lands, and the interest of the Landlord sold therefore.

— Document No. 6 —

ANTIRENTERS IN THE NEW YORK STATE CAMPAIGN OF 1846[6]

After the 1846 election, Horace Greeley, editor of the Whig New York Tribune, *commented on the effectiveness of the Antirenters' political tactics, comparing them to the Liberty Party's policy of naming its own independent candidates. Greeley felt Hamilton Fish, Whig nominee for Lieutenant-Governor, lost the election because the Antirenters believed he sympathized with the landlords.*

The returns and reports from the interior counties of the State leave no doubt of the defeat of the Whig candidate for Lieutenant Governor by some 3 to 6,000 majority. We deeply regret this defeat, most unfortunate for the Whig Cause, and most undeserved by Mr. Fish. . . .

The [*New York*] *Express* says that by nominating differently for Governor, we might have secured (at what cost) the Native vote and so have carried the State *without* the Anti-Renters. This averment assumes that the Anti-Renters would have thrown away their votes on a separate ticket if the Whigs had nominated adversaries of their cause. But nothing supports while everything controverts this assumption. The Anti-Renters have uniformly acted on the rule opposite to that of the Birney Abolitionists—that of taking up the candidate most favorable to their cause whom they could probably elect. They have very rarely thrown away a vote on utterly hopeless candidates. To concentrate their strength and throw it where it would *tell* has been their policy. . . .

When the Anti-Rent State Convention was about to assemble, we learned that Mr. Young would probably be nominated by it for Governor with Mr. Gardner for Lt.

[6] New York *Weekly Tribune,* November 14, 1846.

Governor. We used all the influence we possessed to prevent any such nomination, as did the Editor of the Albany *Evening Journal*. We wished and urged the Anti-Renters to make no nomination, but allow each Anti-Renter to vote as he should see fit. But they chose to pursue their own course, and so make their power decisively felt, and they nominated accordingly.

We still hoped that the Whig Anti-Renters would vote for Mr. Fish, in sufficient numbers to secure his election. We made some effort to secure that result. All in vain, however. The ferocious denunciations of the Anti-Renters *en masse* by the *Courier & Enquirer*, which openly opposed Mr. Young but professed zealously to support Mr. Fish, with the corresponding but less manly course of the *Express*, paralyzed or rendered nugatory every exertion. Mr. Fish was regarded throughout the Anti-Rent District as the candidate of Patroonery,—of those who denounce the Anti-Renters indiscriminately as outlaws, robbers and murderers—of those who had tried to bully the Whig party by threatening to bolt and to draw off 30,000 votes if any 'radical of *The Tribune* school' should be nominated for Governor.

— Document No. 7 —

ADDRESS AND PLATFORM OF THE NATIVE AMERICAN PARTY, JULY 4, 1845 [7]

On July 4, 1845, in a convention at Philadelphia, political Nativists made their first attempt to form a nationwide "Native American" party. At this time the delegates adopted an address and set of resolutions setting forth Nativist doctrines that changed but little during the next decade, when a stronger anti-foreign movement took form

[7] Hector Orr, editor, *The Native American* (Philadelphia, 1845), pp. 145-165.

in the Know-Nothing party. The convention made no
presidential nomination for the 1848 election.

✓   ✓   ✓

The body of foreign citizens, invited to our shores under
a constitutional provision adapted to other times and other
political conditions of the world, and of this country especially, has been endowed by American hospitality, with
gratuitous privileges unnecessary to the enjoyment of those
inalienable rights of man—life, liberty, and the pursuit of
happiness;—privileges wisely reserved to the natives of
the soil, by the governments of all other civilized nations. . . .

In former years, this body was recruited chiefly from
the victims of political oppression, or the active and intelligent mercantile adventurers of other lands; and it
then constituted a slender representation of the best classes
of the foreign population, well fitted to add strength to the
state, and capable of being readily educated in the pecul-
iarly American science of political self-government. Moreover, while welcoming the stranger of every condition,
our laws then wisely demanded of every foreign aspirant
for political rights *a certificate of practical good citizen-*
ship. Such a class of aliens were followed by no foreign
demagogues—they were courted by no domestic demagogues—they were purchased by no parties—they were
debauched by no emissaries of kings. A wall of fire separated them from such a baneful influence, erected by their
intelligence, their knowledge, their virtue and love of
freedom. But for the last twenty years, the road to civil
preferment and participation in the legislative and executive government of the land has been laid broadly open,
alike to the ignorant, the vicious and the criminal; and a
large proportion of the foreign body of citizens and
voters now constitutes a representation of the worst and
most degraded of the European population—victims of
social oppression or personal vices, utterly divested by
ignorance or crime, of the moral and intellectual requisites
for political self-government.

Thus tempted by the suicidal policy of these United
States, and favored by the facilities resulting from the
modern improvements of navigation, numerous societies
and corporate bodies in foreign countries have found it

economical to transport to our shores at public and private expense, the feeble, the imbecile, the idle and intractable, thus relieving the burdens resulting from the vices of the European social systems, by availing themselves of the generous errors of our own. . . .

The mass of foreign voters, formerly lost among the natives of the soil, has increased from the ratio of one in forty to one in seven! A like advance in fifteen years will leave the native citizens a minority in their own land! Thirty years ago these strangers came by units and by tens—now they swarm by thousands. Formerly, most of them sought only for an honest livelihood and a provision for their families; and rarely meddled with those institutions of which it was impossible that they could comprehend the nature; *now* each new comer seeks political preferment, and struggles to fasten on the public purse, with an avidity, in strict proportion to his ignorance and unworthiness of public trust—having been SENT for the purpose of obtaining political ascendancy in the government to the nation—having been SENT to exalt their allies to power—having been SENT to work a revolution from republican freedom to the 'divine right' of monarchs. . . .

The body of adopted citizens with foreign interests and prejudices, is annually advancing, with rapid strides, in geometrical progression. Already it has acquired a control of our elections which cannot be entirely corrected even by the wisest legislation, until the present generation shall be numbered with the past. Already it has notoriously swayed the course of national legislation, and invaded the purity of local justice.—In a few years its unchecked progress would cause it to outnumber the native defenders of our rights, and would then inevitably dispossess *our* offspring, and its own, of the inheritance for which *our fathers bled,* or plunge this land of happiness and peace into the horrors of a civil war.

The correction of these evils can never be effected by any combination governed by the tactics of other existing parties. If either of the old parties, as such, were to attempt an extension of the term of naturalization, it would be impossible for them to carry out the measure, because they would immediately be abandoned by the foreign voters. This great measure can be carried out only by an organization like our own, made up of those who have given up their former political preferences.

For these reasons, we recommend the immediate organization of the truly patriotic native citizens throughout the United States, for the purpose of resisting the progress of foreign influence in the conduct of American affairs, and the correction of such political abuses as have resulted from unguarded or partisan legislation on the subject of naturalization . . . and in furtherance of this object, we present the public with the following statement of the political principles and objects of the Native American body, whose duly constituted representatives we are.

Principles

We hold that, with few exceptions, no man educated under one system of government can ever become thoroughly imbued with the essence and spirit of another system essentially different in character.

That no man can eradicate entirely the prejudices and attachments associated with the land of his birth, so as to become a perfectly safe depository for political trust in any other country.

That the obligation of an oath of fealty to a foreign nation has been decided, by every civilized nation but our own, to be of secondary power when brought into collision with the natural fealty due to the native land. And although we have as yet no absolute decision of this question in our Supreme Court, all precedents bearing on the subject lead us to anticipate a similar conclusion there.

And therefore:—That the elective franchise, which is the primary and fundamental element of popular sovereignty, can only be entirely secure when held exclusively in the hands of natives of the soil.

But, in consideration of the present and previous policy of our government, we are willing, at present, to extend as a boon, to all peaceful and well disposed strangers hereafter settling among us, not only every security enjoyed by the native in the protection of person, property, and the legal pursuit of happiness, but also the right of suffrage, UPON THE SAME TERMS AS THOSE IMPOSED UPON THE NATIVES; namely, a legally authenticated residence of at least twenty-one years within the limits of the country. . . .

We stand pledged, in the exercise of our constitutional right of selecting those candidates for office whom we esteem most capable and best informed; to confine our political nominations to the native-born citizens of the United States, including such foreign-born citizens, only, as may have been parties to the Federal Constitution at the time of its adoption.

We solemnly protest against all intermingling of national policy with the local policy of particular States, on questions involving the reserved rights of those States. . . .

If it is asked what measures of public import we most favor as a party, we answer—all that stand high as American measures, in contradistinction to foreign. Native agriculture we cherish first—native industry, first and last, in every branch of trade—art—ingenuity—mechanics —and invention. We aim at the independence of our country—in all things—moral, intellectual, physical, and political—in works of the hand, as well as in works of the head—in manual labor and in mental sagacity. We desire to make our government what our fathers designed it should be—and witness native statesmen in power— native industry triumphant over foreign labor—and native hearts, announcing America emancipated from all the world.

— Document No. 8 —

FLOURNOY'S LETTER OF ACCEPTANCE, MARCH 22, 1855 [8]

Thomas S. Flournoy, a lawyer, former Whig Congressman, and personally popular Virginia aristocrat, was named by the Know-Nothings as their candidate for the

[8] James P. Hambleton, *A Biographical Sketch of Henry A. Wise, with a History of the Political Campaign in Virginia in 1855* (Richmond, Virginia, 1856), pp. 169-171.

governorship of the Old Dominion in 1855. In his letter of acceptance, Flournoy, a strong Unionist, echoed the South's fears of the large foreign immigration which was adding greatly to the growth of the North and destroying the balance of power between that section and the South.

    ✓   ✓   ✓

Halifax Court House, March 22, 1855

Gentlemen:

I have just received your letter of the 14th, informing me of my nomination by the Convention at Winchester, for the office of Governor of this State, and requesting my acceptance.

It was well known to all who communicated with me upon the subject, that for reasons entirely personal to myself, I had no desire to occupy such a position. . . . But my entire confidence in and earnest desire for the success of the principles of that party, upon which, in my humble judgment, depend the protection of the rights of the States, and the preservation of the Union, induce me to accept the nomination.

In doing so, it is proper that I shall express my opinions upon the subjects which most interest the people of the State.

I am in favor of a general system of popular education.

I am in favor of completing the leading lines of internal improvement, now under prosecution, with as much dispatch as the financial condition of the State will justify, keeping always in view the preservation of her faith and credit.

I endorse fully the Basis of Principles of the American party, believing them to be the most conservative presented to the consideration of the country since the establishment of our independence.

The rapid increase of foreign immigration is well calculated to excite alarm, and the power of the Government, both State and Federal, should be exerted to check it. It seems almost impossible to doubt that the influx of between four and five hundred thousand foreigners into our country annually, will ultimately be subversive of our Republican institutions. Washington, Jefferson, Madison and Jackson gave early warning to the country of the danger to be apprehended from foreign influence. The naturalization laws should either be repealed or so modified, and such restrictions imposed as to avert the evil.

The South is especially and deeply interested in this question. This immense annual addition to our population settle in the non-slaveholding States and the extensive territories of the West and Northwest, out of which Free States will, in consequence, be more speedily formed, increasing with fearful rapidity the balance of power against us.

Intimately connected with this question of foreign immigration, is the growth of the Roman Catholic Church in our country. Despotic, proscriptive, and intolerant, its ascendancy, as all history teaches, has ever been destructive of freedom of opinion, and while I would uncompromisingly oppose any interference with the rights of its members as citizens, by any legislative enactment, yet by a full and independent exercise of the right of suffrage and the appointing power, they should be excluded from the offices of the Government in all its departments.

It may be said that there are comparatively but few foreigners and Roman Catholics in Virginia. She is not acting for herself alone. She is a leading member of this great sisterhood of States, and her action will be felt for weal or woe, by them all. Her destiny is identified with theirs, and she cannot look with indifference to the fact, that the great valley of the Mississippi, watered by twenty thousand miles of navigable rivers, and the immense and fertile Territories, stretching beyond to the Pacific, capable of sustaining a population of one hundred millions, are rapidly filling up with this class of people.

I will advert particularly to one other principle of the American party—the "non-intervention of the Federal and State government with the municipal affairs of each other." The strict observance of this principle will make the union of the States perpetual. . . .

If with these opinions, and this position, the people of Virginia shall elect me to the distinguished office of Governor of the Commonwealth. . . . I will endeavor to advance the prosperity, guard the honor, and protect the interests and institutions of Virginia . . . , and I shall do all that I can consistently with her interest and honor for the preservation of the Union.

— Document No. 9 —

GOVERNOR HENRY J. GARDNER'S ADDRESS TO THE MASSACHUSETTS LEGISLATURE, JANUARY 9, 1857[9]

From 1855 to 1858, Massachusetts was governed by Know-Nothings; the Nativists' gubernatorial candidate, Henry J. Gardner, ran successfully from 1854-1857, while in 1855 and 1856 Know-Nothings won controlling majorities in both houses of the legislature. In this address Gardner interpreted the mission of New England Nativism and sought to show how immigrants had thwarted this mission by their vote in the 1856 presidential campaign.

✓   ✓   ✓

GENTLEMEN OF THE SENATE AND HOUSE OF REPRESENTATIVES:—

Our nation has just passed through another Presidential contest under circumstances which would have imperilled the existence of any other government on the globe; and yet, so admirably harmonious are the workings of our system, and so readily obedient are our people to the will of the majority, that a stranger among us would hardly have supposed so momentous an event had transpired, as the struggle between antagonistic theories concerning the administration of our government, which, thought nominally for the term of four years, nevertheless may tell upon its policy and destiny for generations. And though nowhere was the result so great a disappointment to so

[9] *Massachusetts Executive Documents,* 1857, no. 3, pp. 1-9.

large a proportion of our citizens as in Massachusetts, and nowhere was the real magnitude of the issue more fully appreciated, and hopes of a different termination more earnestly indulged, yet here, with a firm reliance on the ultimate triumph of the great principles we cherish, our people acquiesce in the result in the proper spirit of our institutions. Yet, though as patriots and good citizens we submit to the will of the majority, it is not only our right but our duty to examine thoroughly the causes which produced so unfavorable a result—a result not only prejudicial, we fear, to the cause of Freedom, but portending evil to the integrity of our Union—and to strive, as far as we may, legally, justly and honorably, to remove them for the future. . . .

Although it was freely asserted and widely believed that the question of Freedom or Slavery in Kansas would hinge upon the result of this election, and although, had it terminated in a different manner, the probability of her early admission into the Union as a Free State would have been materially strengthened, yet recent developments give strong hopes that the present chief executive officer of that Territory, in contradistinction to his predecessor, will administer the laws fairly and impartially, will protect the actual settlers in their just rights, and will resist the intrusion of non-residents for illegal purposes. Such are the convictions of those on the spot most capable of judging, and most effectively aiding in the accomplishment of these desired purposes. If so, the energy of our citizens in the race of colonization, aided by the individual and associated cooperation of the intellectual influence and material resources of the people of the North, will certainly outstrip the more sluggish tide of Southern emigration, and insure the triumph of free territory in the approaching State of Kansas. . . .

Still, so far as the decision of the Presidential election is final . . . our citizens have the bitter assurance of knowing that that decision has been made, that action fixed, and that step taken, by the casting votes of aliens born, aliens unnaturalized, and aliens entirely ignorant of our institutions and grossly callous to the vast interests involved in this stupendous issue. While this horde of foreign-born voters has thus stricken down a noble cause, which appealed to the moral sentiment and enlightened patriotism of our country, it only affords another confirmation of a fact which our whole history establishes, that the foreign vote, with hardly an exception, always has been and in the nature of things ever will and must be, attracted to that party which, under high-sounding generalities on the abstract rights of man, always practically cooperates with Slavery at the South, and banishes from its platform the moral questions, and nobler instincts, and more enlightened sentiments of the age.

All classes of aliens, both high and low, are absorbed, with few exceptions into this extreme and self-styled progressive party, by laws of the human mind as inevitable as they are constant. . . .

With these prepossessions the foreigner lands upon our shores, and irresistibly attaches himself to the party bearing this name he has been taught to worship. So it has been, and so it ever will be. And it is this alien body which has decided in the past, many of our great national elections, and in the future, unless checked, is destined to thwart many of the noblest movements which New England, cooperating with the New England sentiments—morality and education—diffused through the great West, may undertake in behalf of freedom, humanity, and the nobler spirit of the century. It was the deadening influence of this body which counteracted the great Northern uprising of the last national election. For wherever New England sentiments, New England education, and New England morality, by reason of State colonization from the indigenous and unmixed population of these six states, were diffused and predominated, there without an exception, the cause of free territory triumphed. And not only foreign ignorance and vice, but German rationalism, and infidelity of Southern Europe, and the Godless philosophy so prevalent among her educated men and better citizens, bear an instinctive antagonism to the moral sentiment and practical Christianity which underlaid the movement involved in this Presidential contest, and which will underlie all conservative attempts to develop and carry out the genuine American spirit of our republican institutions.

There is but one remedy and but one barrier to this steady and increasing power. I fully discussed this remedy, and the principles which compelled me to advocate its adoption, in my first Message to the Legislature of Massachusetts; and I earnestly reiterate the sentiments therein contained, so signally and so deplorably have they been confirmed by the unmistakable lesson of the events of the past year. And I urge attention to them because it is so strikingly evident that the great battle—of which the contest of 1856 was but the preliminary skirmish—the great battle to keep out of the Union Cuba, Mexico, and Central America, with their aliens and their slaves,—countries blasted by Spanish tyranny and the Inquisition, till they are but the melancholy fragments and relics of States with a degenerate population, and are fit only as lands for the transplanting of Negro Slavery to grow side by side with the grossest political and religious serfdom,—this great battle can be triumphantly fought only by appealing to the people under the banner of the principles I have therein enumerated, which principles are not grounded merely in the passions and prejudices, but commend themselves to the reflective judgment of our citizens. . . .

— Document No. 10 —

JOSHUA LEAVITT DEFINES THE PURPOSE OF A POLITICAL ANTISLAVERY ORGANIZATION, JULY 15, 1841 [10]

When a few abolitionists first broached the subject of an Antislavery political party, many of their associates protested that such a step would cost Abolitionism its moral support. Political action, they felt, was just another issue like women's rights and peace that would divide Abolitionist ranks. In the following editorial Joshua Leavitt, one of the leading advocates of political action,

---

[10] *The Emancipator* (Boston), July 15, 1841.

*dealt with this objection and then explained the object of
an Antislavery party.*

✓   ✓   ✓

We have never sought to change our present anti-slavery
organization, with its machinery of national, state, and
county societies, into a political association. In enforcing
the duty of political abolition-action, our appeals have been
made to abolitionists, in their *unorganized* capacity. We
have called upon them to exercise the power of voting
against slavery, not as Abolitionists . . . , but as citizens,
having individually certain duties to perform in behalf of
human rights. In the East this distinction has not been so
carefully maintained; the principle advocates of independent nominations indeed lay no stress upon it, but call
upon anti-slavery *societies* to act, as political bodies. . . .

More importance is attached to this distinction than
many at first sight suppose. The object of our societies is,
the extinction of slavery in the United States. No legitimate objection can be urged to them so long as they
pursue this great object by moral means, technically so
called. But, their transformation into political caucusses
or societies, still maintaining the same object, would, to
say the least, give them an alarming aspect, and confirm
the suspicions of the South, that we are determined to use
the political power of the United States, in contravention
of the constitution, for the accomplishment of our ends.

This leads us to say, that the proper object of political
anti-slavery action in the free states is *not,* to abolish
slavery in the South—for the best of all reasons—we have
no political power by the constitution which can reach
that evil. Hence, the manifest propriety of keeping our
political action separate from our societies. As citizens of
the free states we may organize politically for what object
we please, within constitutional limits. What then is the
legitimate object of political antislavery action? . . . It
is, to disenthrall the laws, institutions and politics of the
free states from subjection to slavery influence; to rid
these states of all responsibility in upholding the system
of slavery; to give such power to the anti-slavery element
in the general government as shall be sufficient to free
domestic and foreign policy of the United States, from
slaveholding control, and withdraw all federal support,

not absolutely demanded by the constitution, from the system of slavery. . . .

We must suppress slavery in the District of Columbia, and the domestic slave-trade; we must seek an amendment of the constitution so as to relieve ourselves from the engagement to surrender up fugitive slaves.

— Document No. 11 —

RESOLUTIONS OF A MASSACHUSETTS CONVENTION OF FRIENDS OF INDEPENDENT ANTISLAVERY NOMINATIONS, SEPTEMBER 11, 1840[11]

Taking advantage of the after-effects of the Panic of 1837, Liberty Party adherents began to point to the dangers slavery posed to the Northern economy, and suggested innumerable financial advantages that the whole country would gain from the abolition of the Southern wage system. This set of resolutions passed by a Massachusetts Liberty Party convention was typical of statements issued by similar meetings throughout the North during the early 1840's.

Resolved, That the election of Harrison and Tyler, Van Buren and Johnson, or any other slaveholder or defender of slavery or any other person, who will make the mere question of interest on which the old parties divide, paramount to the abolition of slavery, involves of necessity a sacrifice of every principle of public and private right, and morality, to secure the perpetuity and profitableness

[11] *The Emancipator* (Boston), November 5, 1840.

of the system of colored and unpaid labor: . . . and whereas, as a mere question of interest the abolition of slavery would ensure to labor its reward; and whereas, it would extend the cultivation of the great staples of the South, by the introduction of machinery, and improved systems of cultivation; and whereas, it would open to the emigrant *free laborers* the vast portion of the South which cannot be reclaimed by slave labor; and whereas, it would remove disgrace from agricultural, mechanical, and domestic labor, and thus invite the enterprising to pursue them; and whereas, it would increase the amount of productive labor from the colored, and the number of producers from the white race, and thus add to the resources of the community and increase the number of consumers, so as to double and treble the demand for the manufactures and agriculture and mechanical productions of the northern States, and thus secure great advantages to the northern laborer and capitalist; and whereas, it would remove the chief cause of the uncertain and fluctuating legislation of our government, on the great question of finance and revenue, in the unequal value, and necessary conflicting interests of free and slave labor, and thus give more security to the relation of northern creditors and southern debtors; and whereas, it would give greater security to life and property, and secure more respect to individual and social rights; therefore,

Resolved, that the abolition of slavery would do more to facilitate the acquisition of wealth, and promote every interest of the North and of our country, than the most successful issue of the schemes of the whig and democratic parties could do; and, therefore, to refuse to lay aside whig and democratic party feeling, this fall, by not voting for the Liberty ticket, is not only to violate the great law of right, but to disregard those very claims of pecuniary interests, for which duty and freedom are to be sacrificed. . . .

— Document No. 12 —

NEW YORK BARNBURNERS AND THE FREE SOIL CONVENTION OF AUGUST 9, 1848[12]

When the Free Soilers met in convention at Buffalo, New York in 1848 to select a candidate for the presidential election, they could hardly afford to ignore the New York Barnburner nominee, Martin Van Buren. At least a week before the convention met, William Cullen Bryant, poet and Barnburner, editor of the New York Evening Post, *made it clear that the Free Soilers could nominate someone other than Van Buren only at the cost of losing the New York vote.*

✦ ✦ ✦

The Buffalo Convention of the friends of free soil will assemble next Tuesday. . . . According to present appearances, we should judge that the convention will nominate Mr. Van Buren for the presidency. Who will receive the nomination of Vice President, we cannot say. If, however, the convention should not agree upon Mr. Van Buren, and some other name should be laid by it before the country, it will be for the democratic delegates from this State to consider how they may give it to be understood that they do not concur in the proceeding. We say the democratic delegates from this State; for it is only these which will be at all embarrassed by any possible result of the convention. The democrats of New York have already acted in this matter; they have held their convention, and nominated their candidate—nominated him at an early period, before this movement had extended to other States; that candidate has given them to understand that

[12] New York *Evening Post,* reprinted in the Washington *Union,* Aug 4, 1848.

137

he allows this use of his name, and the great mass of the democratic party have thought of no other course than to give him their support.

In deputing any of their fellow-citizens to attend the Buffalo Convention, they have not authorized them to undo the work of the Utica Convention. They might concur in the nomination of a Vice President, and in the expression of opinion concerning the extension of slavery; but they would have no warrant to set aside the candidate agreed upon at Utica, any more than they have to revoke the declaration of principles made there.

The convention, we freely admit, is under no obligation to nominate Mr. Van Buren; but we are not discussing that point. The convention, probably, may nominate a candidate who would be more acceptable to some of the States in which the free-soil party are likely to have a majority. But they cannot, we are confident, nominate any other candidate who would carry the State of New York. Any assent which our delegates might give to the substitution of any other candidate would only dissatisfy the people whom they represent, without carrying them over to his support.

It will be for the convention to consider whether it is worth while to nominate any candidate for whom the powerful vote of the State of New York, where the free-soil movement first took form and consistency, where it has its most complete organization, and where it finds its most numerous champions, cannot be obtained.

We make these remarks in perfect respect to the convention, and with a full admission of its right to dispose of the subject, except so far as New York is concerned, in any manner it may see fit. Our remarks, we trust, will be received in the same spirit in which they are written.

— Document No. 13 —

AN ANTISLAVERY EDITOR COMMENTS ON THE 1852 ELECTION, DECEMBER 9, 1852[13]

In 1847 Gamaliel Bailey, Cincinnati Antislavery newspaper editor, moved to Washington to become editor-in-chief of the National Era, *organ of the American and Foreign Antislavery Society. Although Bailey maintained that he was not a Liberty Party man, he supported the organization and its successor, the Free Soil Party. However, in an editorial he indicated his disapproval of Free Soil coalitions and criticized the motives of many who participated in the party's 1848 campaign.*

✓   ✓   ✓

The [*New York*] *Journal of Commerce,* and other papers of that stamp, compare the Free Democratic vote of 1852 with the Free Soil vote of 1848, when Mr. Van Buren received 291,678. The comparison is unfair. That vote notoriously was not a clear Anti-Slavery vote. A very large proportion of it was composed of seceders from the Democratic party—some, on the ground of principle, some, from personal motives; comparatively few comprehended the true nature of the Anti-slavery movement. Two-fifths of all the votes were in fact given by the anti-Cass men of the State of New York, and the majority of these subsequently reunited with their old associates. The true comparison, therefore, is between 1852 and 1844; and this shows an increase of 92,000.

After the contest of 1844, the Anti-Slavery men relaxed their efforts, and their organization generally was enfeebled. The excitements of the campaign of 1848 aroused

[13] *The National Era* (Washington, D. C.), December 9, 1852.

them, and their organization was merged in the irregular movement of 1848. That movement, though it increased their political power, and gave a more practical direction to their efforts, embarrassed them in some of the States, by entangling them with one of the old parties. In Wisconsin, Vermont, and New York, they were merged in the Democratic Party, and in this way prevented from acting independently with the vigor which might otherwise have characterized their movements. The retrograde policy of the Radical Democrats, or Barnburners, so called, embarrassed in fact the whole organization, and it was not till the year preceding the late election, that the political Anti-Slavery men, or the Free Democracy, began in earnest the work of a separate National organization. The result showed their sagacity. The old parties basely passed under the yoke of Slavery, but the Free Democracy stood, erect and independent. The fact that, in so short a time, they were able to disentangle themselves from all connection with them, and after a short canvass, cast over one hundred and fifty thousand votes for Freedom—an increase of ninety-two thousand over the vote of 1844—is evidence that they embody the elements of power and progress.

— Document No. 14 —

PROHIBITION PLATFORM, JULY 10, 1912 [14]

Throughout its history, the Prohibition Party consistently has lived up to its title and demanded the repeal of all laws legalizing the manufacture and sale of liquor. It has not, however, restricted itself to this one issue. The Party's platforms emphasize social and moral issues, but

[14] Kirk H. Porter and Donald Bruce Johnson, compilers, *National Party Platforms, 1840-1956* (Urbana, Ill., 1956), pp. 182-183.

the Party often has taken strong positions on current economic and political questions. The platform of 1912 illustrates this characteristic of the Prohibitionists.

✓   ✓   ✓

The Prohibition Party in National Convention at Atlantic City, New Jersey, July 10, 1912, recognizing God as the source of all governmental authority, makes the following declarations of principles and policies:

1. The alcoholic drink traffic is wrong; is the most serious drain on the wealth and resources of the nation; is detrimental to the general welfare and destructive of the inalienable rights of life, liberty and the pursuit of happiness. All laws taxing or licensing a traffic which produces crime, poverty and political corruption, and spreads disease and death should be repealed. To destroy such a traffic there must be elected to power a political party which will administer the government from the standpoint that the alcoholic drink traffic is a crime and not a business, and we pledge that the manufacture, importation, exportation, transportation and sale of alcoholic beverages shall be prohibited.

We favor:

2. Suffrage for women on the same terms as for men.

3. A uniform marriage and divorce law. The extermination of polygamy. And the complete suppression of the traffic in girls.

4. Absolute protection of the rights of labor, without impairment of the rights of capital.

5. The settlement of all international disputes by arbitration.

6. The abolition of child labor in mines, workshops, and factories, with the rigid enforcement of the laws now flagrantly violated.

7. The election of the United States Senators by direct vote of the people.

8. A Presidential term of six years, and one term only.

9. Court review of Post Office and other departmental decisions and orders; the extension of the Postal Savings Bank system, and of Rural Delivery, and the establishment of an efficient parcels post.

10. The initiative, referendum, and recall.

11. As the tariff is a commercial question it should be fixed on the scientific basis of accurate knowledge, secured by means of a permanent, omni-partisan tariff commission, with ample powers.

12. Equitable graduated income and inheritance taxes.

13. Conservation of our forest and mineral reserves, and the reclamation of waste lands. All mineral and timber lands, and water powers, now owned by the government, should be held perpetually, and leased for revenue purposes.

14. Clearly defined laws for the regulation and control of corporations transacting an inter-state business.

15. Efficiency and economy in governmental administration.

16. The protection of one day in seven as a day of rest.

To these fundamental principles, the National Prohibition Party renews its long allegiance, and on these issues invites the co-operation of all good citizens, to the end that the true object of government may be attained, namely, equal and exact justice for all.

— Document No. 15 —

JAMES B. WEAVER'S LETTER OF ACCEPTANCE AS GREENBACK PRESIDENTIAL NOMINEE, JULY 3, 1880 [15]

The National Greenback convention of June 9, 1880, was made up of delegates representing all shades of radical opinion. Socialists and woman suffrage supporters mingled with Greenbackers who were themselves divided

[15] *The Platform of the National Greenback Labor Party and the letter of Acceptance of General J. B. Weaver* (leaflet, n.p., n.d.)

over the advisability of fusion with the Democrats. Although Benjamin F. Butler of Massachusetts and Edward P. Allis of Wisconsin were mentioned as possible candidates, James B. Weaver of Iowa received the nomination on the first ballot. On July 3, Weaver sent the following letter accepting the nomination and declaring his approval of the Greenback platform.

✓   ✓   ✓

GENTLEMEN: It is my pleasure to acknowledge the receipt of your letter of June 23, 1880, formally notifying me of my nomination for the office of President of the United States, by the united Greenback Labor Party, whose representatives convened at Chicago, June 9th, 1880.

I am profoundly grateful for the honor conferred. Fully realizing the high responsibility to which I have been called, and conscious that the position was unsought by me, I accept the nomination as a solemn duty. The convention is to be congratulated upon the great work accomplished in the unification of the various Greenback and Labor elements into one compact organization. This was of first importance, and thoroughly prepares our forces to strike a decisive blow for industrial emancipation during the impending struggle.

Our party hath this significance; it is a great labor movement, composed of earnest people, who earn their bread by honest toil whether of hand, head or heart; and as the world depends for the comforts of life upon the various departments of human toil, so will every part of society feel the vivifying influence of the grand achievements of our organization that lie just in the future; for when labor is prosperous, every other element of society feels the impulse of vigorous life.

The three great political parties have each selected their candidates and made formal declaration of their principles. It is now the high duty of every citizen of the United States to judge between them; and after careful inquiry into the aims and purposes of each, to determine the organization, with which duty calls him to act. . . .

It being the duty of man to earn his bread in the sweat of his face, it becomes the first duty of civil government to foster industry. All laws, therefore, which place a premium upon idleness, whether of men or money, unjustly discriminate in favor of capital, or withhold from honest men the full and just reward of their labor, are simply monstrous. Capital should be the servant of labor rather than its master.

The great truth can never be realized until there is an adequate circulating medium. Inasmuch as this circulating medium is for the benefit of all, its issue and volume should be sacredly kept under the control of the people, without the intervention of banking corporations. . . .

The system which now prevails, gives into the hands of banking corporations absolute control over the volume of the currency, and through this they have the power to fix the price of the labor and property of fifty millions of people. . . .

There are three industrial classes in America: First, the producers; second, those who manufacture our raw materials and prepare them for use; third, the distributers of these products. Each should be protected in the legitimate fruits and profits of their labor, but should not be permitted to extort from and enslave the others.

The great problem of our civilization is, how to bring the producer and consumer together. This can only be done by providing an adequate circulating medium, and by rigid regulation of inter-State commerce and transportation. . . .

The two great agents of commerce are money and transportation. It is undeniable that both of these agents are under absolute control of monopolies. . . .

This places the people between the upper and nether millstones, and grinds them to poverty and ruin. It results in the wholesale robbery of both producer and consumer. . . .

An area of our public domain, larger than the territory occupied by the great German empire, has been wantonly donated to wealthy corporations; while a bill introduced by Hon. Hendrick B. Wright, of Pennsylvania, to enable our poor people to reach and occupy the few acres remaining, has been scouted, ridiculed, and defeated in Congress. In consequence of this stupendous system of land grabbing, millions of the young men of America, and millions more of industrious people from abroad, seeking homes in the New World, are left homeless and destitute. The public domain must be sacredly reserved to actual settlers, and where corporations have not complied strictly with the terms of their grants, the land should be at once reclaimed.

The immigration of persons from foreign countries, seeking homes and desiring to become citizens of the United States, should be encouraged, but the importation of Chinese servile laborers should be prohibited by stringent laws. . . .

One of the grand missions of our party is to banish forever from American politics that deplorable spirit of sectional hatred, which, for base purposes, has been fostered by the leaders of the old parties. This has greatly deceived and embittered the public mind, both North and South.

Our civilization demands a new party, dedicated to the pursuits of peace, and which will not allow the war issues ever to be re-opened, and will render the military strictly subordinate to the civil power. The war is over, and the sweet voice of peace, long neglected, calls us to worship at her altars. Let us crowd her temples with willing votaries. Let us have a free ballot, a fair count, and equal rights for all classes—for the laboring man in Northern manufactories, mines, and workshops, and for the struggling poor, both white and black, in the cotton fields of the South.

I most earnestly and solemnly invoke united action of all industrial classes, irrespective of party, that we may make a manly struggle for the independence of labor, and to re-establish in the administration of public affairs the old-time Democracy of Jefferson and Jackson, and the pure Republicanism of Abraham Lincoln and Thaddeus Stevens. . . .

And now, eschewing all violence and tumult as unworthy of the cause we represent, and relying upon Divine Providence and the justice of our cause, let us go forth in the great struggle for human rights.

With high regard, I am, your obedient servant.

J. B. WEAVER

A LABOR ORGANIZER'S PLAN FOR BUILDING AN EFFECTIVE THIRD PARTY IN 1888 [16]

Joseph R. Buchanan, an ardent trade-unionist and labor editor, participated in labor and reform politics during the last two decades of the 19th century. Though a socialist in principle, his search for an effective political combination carried him in and out of many radical and reform organizations. In this extract from his autobiography, Buchanan comments on the problems of building a strong third party out of the diverse reform elements of the 1880's, and presents his own solution to the dilemma.

✓   ✓   ✓

The beginning of the year 1888 found the political atmosphere filled with rumors of parties, the mission of each and every one of which would be to wipe the old parties off the face of the earth and secure the establishment of a people's government. Division of the independent political forces into one, two, or half a dozen parties has ever been the bane of progress in this country. During the sixteen years preceding 1888 there had been attempts under a dozen different banners, and upon as many platforms to wrest government (municipal, state and national) from the control of the monopolistic money power of the land. I had taken part in several of these attempts. We had failed utterly in almost every instance; our successes had been insignificant and of no practical benefit. The exploiters of the producers and the politicians had outgeneraled us. Thefts of public lands, credits, and franchises had gone on at a constantly accelerating rate,

[16] Joseph R. Buchanan, *The Story of a Labor Agitator* (New York, 1903) pp. 426-33.

and our puny protests had been laughed to scorn. Realizing that all future efforts, if directed along the lines we had been following, were doomed in advance to failure, I made a suggestion embodying another policy. As my proposal was discussed in hundreds of reform and labor papers throughout the country and accepted by many of them, and as "Buchanan's nine-word platform" was for six months a frequent topic considered by party-makers, —and party breakers,—a portion of the editorial in "The Enquirer" which inaugurated the agitation may interest the reader—

". . . Men representing a dozen different shades of opinion have come together, ostensibly to pool their issues and amalgamate the elements variedly represented. When they have come to write the 'union' platform, each one has insisted upon putting his ideas, every one of them, to the front; and each one claimed that he had the cure-all. There were frequently conflicting propositions; it was impossible to get them all into one platform and make the planks fit in properly. Well, the upshot of the business has been a few truces; the stronger faction has written the platform, while the rest have gone home sore-headed and and—the millionaires have continued to run the machine. . . .

"There must be a union of the following forces: The Union Labor Party, United Labor Party, Progressive Labor Party, American Reform Party, the Grange, the Tax Reformers, the Farmers' Alliance, Anti-Monopolists, Homesteaders, and all other political and politico-economic organizations of bread-winners. How is this amalgamation to be brought about? . . . By putting into it [*the platform*] the one thing that all the elements approve . . . *Government ownership and operation of the railroads and telegraph* . . . . Let each wing of the reform movement withhold for twelve months its hobbies, and all join hands for a united onslaught on one of the enemies' weakest, though most important, points."

As has been said, my nine-word platform, declaring for "Government ownership and operation of the railroads and telegraph" was widely discussed. Reform editors generally indorsed it; but some of the "leading reformers" were not satisfied with the short platform. They liked it, "so far as it goes"; but—. One thought it would be ex-

cellent if it only had a "money plank" added. Another
said it needed just a single-tax plank . . . . Women suffrage, an eight-hour work day, postal savings banks, direct legislation, proportional representation, and a score
of other hobbies, were said by their respective devotees
to be absolutely necessary to make the platform perfect.
The "lumber-shovers" who were responsible for the in-
surmountable piles of misfit planks that past conventions
had denominated "platforms" got to work early. . . .

— Document No. 17 —

DONNELLY'S PREAMBLE TO THE POPULIST PARTY PLATFORM, JULY 4, 1892 [17]

*Ignatius Donnelly of Minnesota, Populism's greatest
orator, drafted this premable first for the St. Louis conference of February, 1892, and presented it again at the
party's nominating convention in July at Omaha. For his
material Donnelly drew heavily on the language of the
February convention call and also on the "Populist Mani-
festo" issued by the Kansas state central committee in
November, 1891. Delegates responded to his peroration
with a wild twenty-five minute demonstration.*

✓   ✓   ✓

Assembled upon the 116th anniversary of the declaration of independence, the People's party of America, in
their first national convention, invoking upon their action
the blessing of Almighty God, puts forth, in the name
and on behalf of the people of this country, the following preamble and declaration of principles:

The conditions which surround us best justify our cooperation: we meet in the midst of a nation brought to
the verge of moral, political and material ruin. Corrup-

tion dominates the ballot-box, the legislatures, the Congress, and touches even the ermine of the bench. The people are demoralized; most of the States have been compelled to isolate the voters at the polling places to prevent universal intimidation or bribery. The newspapers are largely subsidized or muzzled, public opinion silenced, business prostrated, our homes covered with mortgages, labor impoverished, and the land concentrating in the hands of the capitalists. The urban workmen are denied the right of organization for self protection, imported pauperized labor beats down their wages, a hireling standing army, unrecognized by our laws, is established to shoot them down, and they are rapidly degenerating into European conditions. The fruits of the toil of millions are boldly stolen to build up colossal fortunes for a few unprecedented in the history of mankind, and the possessors of these, in turn, despise the republic and endanger liberty. From the same prolific womb of governmental injustice we breed the two great classes—tramps and millionaires.

The national power to create money is appropriated to enrich bondholders; a vast public debt payable in legal tender currency has been funded into gold bearing bonds, thereby adding millions to the burdens of the people.

Silver, which has been accepted as coin since the dawn of history, has been demonetized to add to the purchasing power of gold by decreasing the value of all forms of property as well as human labor, and the supply of currency is purposely abridged to fatten usurers, bankrupt enterprise, and enslave industry. A vast conspiracy against mankind has been organized on two continents, and it is rapidly taking possession of the world. If not met and overthrown at once, it forbodes terrible social convulsions, the destruction of civilization, or the establishment of absolute despotism. We have witnessed for more than a quarter of a century the struggles of the two great political parties for power and plunder, while grievous wrongs have been inflicted upon the suffering people. We charge that the controlling influences dominating both these parties have permitted the existing dreadful conditions to develop without serious effort to prevent or restrain them.

Neither do they now promise us any substantial reform. They have agreed together to ignore, in the coming campaign, every issue but one. They propose to drown the outcries of a plundered people with the uproar of a sham-battle over the tariff, so that capitalists, corporations, national banks, rings, trusts, watered stock, the demonetization of silver and the oppressions of the usurers may all be lost sight of. They propose to sacrifice our homes, lives, and children on the altar of mammon, to destroy the multitude in order to secure corruption funds from the millionaires. Assembled on the anniversary of the birthday of the nation, and filled with the spirit of the grand general and chieftain who established our independence, we seek to restore the government of the republic to the hands of "the plain people" with whose class it originated. We assert our purposes to be identical with the purposes of the national Constitution, to form a more perfect union and establish justice, insure domestic tranquility, provide for the common defense, promote the general welfare, and secure the blessings of liberty for ourselves and our posterity.

We declare that this republic can only endure as a free government while built on the love of the whole people for each other and for the nation; that it cannot be pinned together by bayonets; that the civil war is over and that every passion and resentment which grew out of it must die with it, and that we must be in fact, as we are in name, one united brotherhood of freedom. Our country finds itself confronted by conditions for which there is no precedent in the history of the world. Our annual agricultural productions amount to billions of dollars in value, which must within a few weeks or months be exchanged for billions of dollars worth of commodities consumed in their production; the existing currency supply is wholly inadequate to make this exchange. The results are falling prices, the formation of combines and rings, the impoverishment of the producing class. We pledge ourselves that if given power we will labor to correct these evils by wise and reasonable legislation in accordance with the terms of our platform. . . . We declare, therefore:

First. That the union of the labor forces in the United States this day consummated shall be permanent and perpetual; may its spirit enter into all hearts for the salvation of the republic and the uplifting of mankind.

Second. Wealth belongs to him who creates it, and every dollar taken from industry without an equivalent is robbery. "If any will not work, neither shall he eat." The interests of rural and civic labor are the same; their enemies are identical.

Third. We believe that the time has come when the railroad corporations will either own the people or the people must own the railroads; . . .

We demand a national currency, safe, sound, and flexible, issued by the general government only, a full legal tender for all debts, public and private. . . .

We demand free and unlimited coinage of silver and gold at the present legal ratio of sixteen to one.

We demand that the amount of circulating medium be speedily increased to not less than $50 per capita.

We demand a graduated income tax.

We believe that the money of the country should be kept as much as possible in the hands of the people, and hence we demand that all States and national revenues shall be limited to the necessary expenses of the government, economically and honestly administered.

We demand that postal savings banks be established by the government for the safe deposit of the earnings of the people and to facilitate exchange.

Transportation being a means of exchange and a public necessity, the government should own and operate the railroads in the interests of the people.

The telegraph and telephone, like the post-office system being a necessity in the transmission of news, should be owned and operated by the government in the interests of the people.

The land, including all the natural sources of wealth, is the heritage of the people, and should not be monopolized for speculative purposes, and alien ownership of land should be prohibited. All land now held by railroads and other corporations in excess of their actual needs and all lands now owned by aliens should be reclaimed by the government, and held for actual settlers only. . . .

HENRY DEMAREST LLOYD'S SPEECH DURING THE POPULIST CAMPAIGN IN COOK COUNTY, ILLINOIS, OCTOBER 6, 1894 [18]

Henry Demarest Lloyd, an outstanding critic of monopoly capitalism, worked hard to unite Populists and labor reformers in a single party in Illinois, in order to prove the viability of such an alliance on a larger scale. In a speech delivered in Chicago during the Cook County campaign, Lloyd outlined his doctrine of a "cooperative commonwealth" which aimed at regaining industrial liberty through collective ownership and operation of as many of the means of production and distribution as the public desired. Lloyd hoped to base his projected alliance on this proposal, but despite his efforts the union proved to be unstable and soon collapsed.

✦ ✦ ✦

The Coming Revolution Is Here

We talk about the coming revolution and hope it will be peaceful. The revolution has come. This use of the government of all for the enrichment and aggrandizement of a few is a revolution. It is a revolution which has created the railroad millionaires of this country. To maintain the highways is one of the sacredest functions of the government. Railroads are possible only by the exercise of the still more sacred governmental power of eminent domain, which, when citizens will not sell the

---

[18] *Seven in One: Speeches . . . Delivered Under the Auspices of the People's Party of Chicago* (Chicago, 1894), n.p.

right of way, takes their property through the forms of law by force—none the less by force, because the money value is paid. These sovereign powers of the highway and of eminent domain have been given by you and me, all of us, to our government to be used only for the common and equal benefit of all. Given by all to be used by all, it is a revolution to have made them the perquisite of a few. Only a revolution could have made possible in the speech of a free people such a phrase of a railroad king.

It is a revolution which has given the best parts of the streets that belong to all the people to street-railway syndicates and power companies. It is a revolution which has created national bank millionaires and bond-millionaires, and tariff millionaires, and land-grant millionaires out of the powers you and I delegated to the government of the United States for the equal good of every citizen. The interstate commerce act was passed to put into prison the railroad managers who used their highway power to rob the people, to ruin the merchants and manufacturers whose business they wanted to give to favored shippers. The anti-trust law was passed to put into prison the men who make commerce a conspiracy, to compel the people every day to pay a ransom for their lives. It is a revolution which is using these inter-state and anti-trust laws to prosecute the employees of the railways for exercising their rights as free men to unite for defense against intolerable wrong. It is a revolution which lets the presidents, and managers and owners of the railroads and trusts go free of all punishment for the crimes they are committing; which sends out no process against any of the corporations or corporation men in the American Railway association, while it uses all the powers to send to prison the member of the American Railway union. It is a revolution which is putting the attorneys of corporations into ermine on the bench to be attorneys still.

It is a revolution by which great combinations, using competition to destroy competition, have monopolized entire markets, and as the sole sellers of goods make the people buy dear, and as the sole purchaser of labor make the people sell themselves cheap. Last and deepest and greatest revolution of all is that by which the mines, machinery, factories, currency, land, entrusted to private hands as private property, only as a stewardship, to warm, feed, clothe, serve mankind, are used to make men cold, hungry, naked and destitute. Coal mines shut down to make coal scarce, mills shut down to make goods scarce, currency used to deprive people of the means of exchange, and the railways used to hinder transportation.

Counter Revolution of the People

This is the revolution that has come. With local variation it is world wide, and against it the people are rising world wide in peaceful counter revolutions, in People's parties. It begins now to be seen generally, what a few have been pointing out from the beginning, that the workingmen in organizing to defend themselves have been only pioneers. The power which denied them a fair share of their productions was the same power which is now attacking the consumer, the farmer, and even the fellow capitalist. In organizing against modern capitalism the working men set the example which all the people are now driven by self-preservation to follow. The trades union of the working men was the precursor of the Farmers' Alliance, the grange, and the People's party.

Chicago today leads the van in this great forward movement. Here the workingmen, capitalists, single-taxers and socialists have come together to join forces with each other and with the farmers, as has been done in no other city. Its meetings are attended here by thousands, as you see tonight. It is the most wonderful outburst of popular hope and enthusiasm in the recent politics of this country. Chicago thus leads in numbers and in enthusiasm and in promises of success, because it has led in boldness, and sincerity and thoroughness of reform doctrine. The workingmen of Chicago at the Springfield conference, which was the fountainhead of this tidal wave, stood firm as a rock for the principle, without which the industrial liberties of the people can never be established—the principle that they have the right at their own option to own and operate collectively any or all of the means of production, distribution and exchange. They already own some; they have the right to own as many more as they want. This is the mother principle of the government we already have, and it covers a whole brood of government railroads, telegraphs, telephones, banks, lands, street railways, all the municipalizations in which everywhere the people are giving utterances to their belief that they are the only proper and the only competent administrators of the wealth which they create.

The declaration of independence of 1776 declared that the people felt themselves able to manage for themselves, the government, all of whose powers sprang from them. This declaration of 1894 is the proclamation of the next step to independence. The people have done so well that they will move forward again and manage for themselves some more departments of the commonwealth, all of whose powers sprung from them. The democratization of the government, the democratization of collective industry—they are parts of the one great upward emancipation. The American idea, says Emerson, is emancipation. The cooperative commonwealth is the legitimate offspring and lawful successor of the republic. Our liberties and our wealth are from the people and by the people and both must be for the people. Wealth, like government, is the product of the cooperation of all, and, like government, must be the property of all its creators, not of a privileged few alone. The principles of liberty, equality, union, which rules in the industries we call government, may rule in all industries. Government exists only by the consent of the governed. Business, property, capital, are also governments and must also rest on the consent of the governed. This assertion of the inherent and inalienable right, and ability, of the people to own and operate at their option, any, or all of the wealth they create is the fundamental, irrepressible, and uncompromiseable key note of the crisis, and with this trumpet note you can lead the people through any sacrifice to certain victory.

— Document No. 19 —

DANIEL DE LEON DISCUSSES REFORM AND REVOLUTION, JANUARY 26, 1896[19]

Daniel De Leon, leading doctrinaire Marxist of early American Socialism, joined the Socialist Labor Party in 1890. He refused to recognize the more Americanized, reformist Socialist Party of America, organized in 1901 and led by Eugene V. Debs. De Leon's leadership in the smaller SLP remained unchallenged at the time of his death in 1914. As a Socialist theoretician, De Leon made his first major contribution to his Party in a speech in Boston on January 26, 1896, where he defined the difference between reform and revolution. Socialism, claimed De Leon, could come only through revolution.

✓   ✓   ✓

We hear people talk about the "reform forces," about "evolution" and about "revolution" in ways that are highly mixed. Let us clear up our terms. Reform means a change of externals; revolution—peaceful or bloody, the peacefulness or the bloodiness of it cuts no figure whatever in the essence of the question—means a change from within.

Reform

Take, for instance, a poodle. You can reform him in a lot of ways. You can shave his whole body and leave a tassel at the tip of his tail; you may bore a hole through each ear, and tie a blue bow on one and a red bow on the other; you may put a brass collar around his neck with your initials on, and a trim little blanket on his back; yet, throughout, a poodle he was and a poodle he

[19] New York *Weekly People*, February 23 and March 1, 1896.

remains. Each of these changes probably wrought a corresponding change in the poodle's life. When shorn of
all his hair except a tassel at the tail's tip he was owned
by a wag who probably cared only for the fun he could
get out of his pet; when he appears gaily decked in bows,
probably his young mistress' attachment is of a tenderer
sort; when later we see him in the fancier's outfit, the
treatment he received and the uses he is put to may again
be, and probably are, different. Each of these transforma-
tions or stages may mark a veritable epoch in the poodle's
existence. And yet, essentially, a poodle he was, a poodle
he is, and a poodle he will remain. That is *reform*.

Revolution

But when we look back myriads of years, or project
ourselves into far-future-physical cataclysms, and trace
the development of animal life from the invertebrate to
the vertebrate, from the lizard to the bird, from the quad-
ruped and mammal till we come to the prototype of the
poodle, and finally reach the poodle himself, and so
forward—then do we find radical changes at each step,
changes from within that alter the very essence of his
being, and that put, or will put, upon him each time a
stamp that alters the very system of his existence. That is
revolution.

So with society. Whenever a change leaves the internal
mechanism untouched, we have *reform;* whenever the
internal mechanism is changed, we have *revolution*.

Of course, no internal change is possible without external manifestations. The internal changes denoted by
the revolution or evolution of the lizard into the eagle
are accompanied by external marks. So with society. And
therein lies one of the pitfalls into which dilettanteism
or reformers invariably tumble. They have noticed that
externals change with internals; and they rest satisfied
with mere external changes, without looking behind the
curtain. But of this more presently.

We Socialists are not reformers; we are revolutionists.
We Socialists do not propose to change forms. We care
nothing for forms. We want a change of the inside of the
mechanism of society; let the form take care of itself.
We see in England a crowned monarch; we see in Germany a sceptered emperor; we see in this country an un-

crowned president, and we fail to see any essential difference between Germany, England, or America. That being the case, we are skeptics as to forms. We are like grown children, in the sense that we like to look at the inside of things and find out what is there.

One more preliminary explanation. Socialism is lauded by some as an angelic movement, by others it is decried as a devilish scheme. Hence you find the Gomperses blowing hot and cold on the subject; and Harry Lloyd, with whose capers, to your sorrow, you are more familiar than I, pronouncing himself a Socialist in one place, and in another running Socialism down. Socialism is neither an aspiration of angels, nor a plot of devils. Socialism moves with its feet firmly planted on the ground, and its head not lost in the clouds; it takes Science by the hand, asks her to lead, and goes whithersoever she points. It does not take Science by the hand, saying: "I shall follow you to the end of the road if it please me." No! It takes her by the hand and says: "Withersoever thou leadest, thither am I *bound* to go." We Socialists, consequently, move as intelligent men; we do not mutiny because, instead of having wings, we have arms, and cannot fly as we would wish. . . .

— Document No. 20 —

DEBS BECOMES A SOCIALIST[20]

Presidential candidate of the Socialist Party of America in 1900, 1904, 1908, 1912, and 1920; orator of Socialism —but not its theoretician; loved and respected by all—but unable to secure their votes, Eugene V. Debs became the symbol of American Socialism during the Party's first three decades. In the following essay, written two years after his first Presidential campaign, Debs reviews his activity with organized labor, from the organization of

[20] Eugene V. Debs, "How I Became a Socialist," *The Comrade,* I (April, 1902), pp. 146-148.

locomotive firemen at Terre Haute to the creation of the American Railway Union (of which he became the first President) and relates how he became a Socialist during his imprisonment following the Pullman strike.

✓   ✓   ✓

On the evening of February 27, 1875, the local lodge of the Brotherhood of Locomotive Firemen was organized at Terre Haute, Indiana, by Joshua A. Leach, then grand master, and I was admitted as a charter member and at once chosen secretary. "Old Josh Leach," as he was affectionately called, a typical locomotive fireman of his day, was the founder of the brotherhood, and I was instantly attracted by his rugged honesty, simple manner and homely speech. . . .

My first step was thus taken in organized labor and I felt that a new influence fired my ambition and changed the whole current of my career. I was filled with enthusiasm and my blood fairly leaped in my veins. Day and night I worked for the brotherhood. To see its watchfires glow and observe the increase of its sturdy members were the sunshine and shower of my life. To attend the "meeting" was my supreme joy, and for ten years I was not once absent when the faithful assembled.

At the convention held in Buffalo in 1878 I was chosen associate editor of the magazine, and in 1880 I became grand secretary and treasurer. With all the fire of youth I entered upon the crusade which seemed to fairly glitter with possibilities. . . .

I rode on the engines over mountain and plain, slept in the cabooses and bunks, and was fed from their pails by the swarthy stokers who still nestle close to my heart, and will until it is cold and still.

Through all these years I was nourished at Fountain Proletaire. I drank deeply of its waters and every particle of my tissue became saturated with the spirit of the working class. I had fired an engine and been stung by the exposure and hardship of the rail. I was with them in their weary watches, at the broken engine's side and often helped to bear their bruised and bleeding bodies back to wife and child again. How could I but feel the burden of their wrongs? How could the seed of agitation fail to take deep root in my heart?

And so I was spurred on in the work of organizing, not the firemen merely, but the brakemen, switchmen, telegraphers, shipmen, track-hands, all of them in fact, and as I had now become known as an organizer, the calls came from all sides and there are but few trades I have not helped to organize and less still in whose strikes I have not at some time had a hand.

In 1894 the American Railway Union was organized and a braver body of men never fought the battle of the working class.

Up to this time I had heard but little of Socialism, knew practically nothing about the movement, and what little I did know was not calculated to impress me in its favor. I was bent on the thorough and complete organization of the railroad men and ultimately the whole working class, and all my time and energy were given to that end. . . .

It is useless to say that I had yet to learn the workings of the capitalist system, the resources of its masters and the weakness of its slaves. Indeed, no shadow of a "system" fell athwart my pathway! no thought of ending wage-misery marred my plans. I was too deeply absorbed in perfecting wage-servitude and making it a "thing of beauty and a joy forever."

It all seems very strange to me now, taking a backward look, that my vision was so focalized on a single objective point that I utterly failed to see what now appears as clear as the noonday sun—so clear that I marvel that any workingmen, however dull, uncomprehending, can resist it.

But perhaps it was better so. I was to be baptized in Socialism in the roar of conflict and I thank the gods for reserving to this fitful occasion the fiat, "Let there be light!"—the light that streams in steady radiance upon the broadway to the Socialist republic.

The skirmish lines of the A.R.U. were well advanced. A series of small battles was fought and won without the loss of a man. A number of concessions was made by the corporations rather than risk an encounter. Then came the fight on the Great Northern, short, sharp, and decisive. The victory was complete—the only railroad strike of magnitude ever won by an organization in America.

Next followed the final shock—the Pullman strike—
and the American Railway Union again won, clear and
complete. The combined corporations were paralyzed and
helpless. At this juncture there was delivered, from
wholly unexpected quarters, a swift succession of blows
that blinded me for an instant and then opened wide
my eyes—and in the gleam of every bayonet and the
flash of every rifle *the class struggle was revealed*. This
was my first practical lesson in Socialism, though wholly
unaware that it was called by that name.

An army of detectives, thugs and murderers was
equipped with badge and beer and bludgeon and turned
loose; old hulks of cars were fired; the alarm bells tolled;
the people were terrified; the most startling rumors were
set afloat; the press volleyed and thundered, and over
all the wires sped the news that Chicago's white throat
was in the clutch of a red mob; injunctions flew thick
and fast, arrests followed, and our office and headquarters, the heart of the strike, was sacked, torn out
and nailed up by the "lawful" authorities of the federal
government; and when in company with my loyal com-
rades I found myself in Cook County jail at Chicago
with the whole press screaming conspiracy, treason and
murder, and by some fateful coincidence I was given
the cell occupied just previous to his execution by the
assassin of Mayor Carter Harrison, Sr., overlooking the
spot, a few feet distant, where the anarchists were hanged
a few years before, I had another exceedingly practical
and impressive lesson in Socialism.

Acting upon the advice of friends we sought to employ John Harlan, son of the Supreme Justice, to assist
in our defense—a defense memorable to me chiefly because of the skill and fidelity of our lawyers, among
whom were the brilliant Clarence Darrow and the venerable Judge Lyman Trumbull, author of the thirteenth
amendment to the constitution, abolishing slavery in the
United States.

Mr. Harlan wanted to think of the matter over night;
and the next morning gravely informed us that he could
not afford to be identified with the case, "for," said he,
"you will be tried upon the same theory as were the
anarchists, with probably the same result." That day, I
remember, the jailer, by way of consolation, I suppose,

showed us the blood-stained rope used at the last execution and explained in minutest detail, as he exhibited the gruesome relic, just how the monstrous crime of lawful murder is committed.

But the tempest gradually subsided and with it the bloodthirstiness of the press and the "public sentiment." We were not sentenced to the gallows, nor even to the penitentiary—though put on trial for conspiracy—for reasons that will make another story.

The Chicago jail sentences were followed by six months at Woodstock and it was here that Socialism gradually laid hold of me in its own irresistible fashion. Books and pamphlets and letters from Socialists came by every mail and I began to read and think and dissect the anatomy of the system in which workingmen, however organized, could be shattered and battered and splintered at a single stroke. The writings of Bellamy and Blatchford early appealed to me. The "Co-operative Commonwealth" of Gronlund also impressed me, but the writings of Kautsky were so clear and conclusive that I readily grasped, not merely his argument, but also caught the spirit of his Socialist utterance—and I thank him and all who helped me out of darkness into light.

It was at this time, when the first glimmerings of Socialism were beginning to penetrate, that Victor L. Berger —and I have loved him ever since—came to Woodstock, as if a providential instrument, and delivered the first impassioned message of Socialism I had ever heard—the very first to set the "wires humming in my system." As a souvenir of that visit there is in my library a volume of "Capital," by Karl Marx, inscribed with the compliments of Victor L. Berger, which I cherish as a token of priceless value.

The American Railway Union was defeated but not conquered—overwhelmed but not destroyed. It lives and pulsates in the Socialist movement, and its defeat but blazed the way to economic freedom and hastened the dawn of human brotherhood.

— Document No. 21 —

THEODORE ROOSEVELT SEEKS THE REPUBLICAN NOMINATION AS A PROGRESSIVE, 1912[21]

While the National Progressive Republican League, organized in 1911, was working to promote Robert M. La Follette as the Republican party's presidential candidate in 1912, ex-President Theodore Roosevelt decided to seek the same nomination. Republican insurgents divided over these two men, and eventually Roosevelt took over most of the support that Progressives had first given to La Follette. In his Autobiography *the Wisconsin senator discussed the sources of the financial support of Roosevelt's campaign.*

But Progressive sentiment was crystallizing about my candidacy so rapidly that the near friends of Roosevelt who had been professing loyalty to me, while at heart for him, were being forced by developments more and more to disclose their real design. And we were fast approaching a time when Roosevelt himself would have to show his hand.

On the nineteenth of January Mr. Homer Mann, chairman of the Fifth District Congressional Committee, called a meeting of party workers together in Kansas City, to whom he said: "Some time ago I wrote to Mr. Roosevelt telling him that it was impossible to carry the state unless he again assumed the leadership of the party. I got a reply. I am not at liberty to give the answer now, but it suffices to say that this meeting was called."

[21] Robert M. La Follette, *La Follette's Autobiography* (Madison, Wisconsin, 1960), pp. 246-249.

I had spoken many times in Kansas. Some three years before [*Joseph L.*] Bristow became a candidate for the United States Senate I had urged my audiences to elect him to succeed Senator [*Chester I.*] Long, and in my meetings throughout the state had reviewed Long's senatorial record. Finally, when Bristow did become a candidate, I had gone to Kansas on the urgent call of William Allen White to speak for Bristow. I had every reason to believe that White, who is very strong in Kansas, was supporting my candidacy.

On the ninth of January a letter was received at our headquarters in Washington from Rodney A. Elward of Castleton, Kansas, an old Wisconsin University friend and supporter of mine, and at present one of the regents of the Kansas State University. In this letter Elward said: "I received a letter from William Allen White this morning saying he is for La Follette."

This letter of White's must have been written a day or two before and about the time I had concluded my tour of Ohio, Michigan, and Illinois.

I was amazed to see it followed on the tenth of January by an editorial in White's paper, the *Emporia Gazette,* concluding an appeal to Progressives to organize for Roosevelt, with the words, "Roosevelt or bust!"

What came to White in that brief interval to change his attitude, I do not know.

The day after the publication of Mr. White's "Roosevelt or bust" editorial, Frank A. Munsey, owner of several newspapers and periodicals, very much interested in the United States Steel Corporation, and one of Roosevelt's financial backers and intimates, published in large type a double column signed editorial on the front page of his papers, of which the following is the concluding paragraph: "Situated as he is, my guess is that Mr. Roosevelt is quite content to let political matters shape themselves up as they will. If no call comes to him to lead the fight, he will keep right on having a good time with his work, as he is now doing. But if the call does come, he will buckle on his armour and 'go to it' with all his old-time impetuosity and energy."

In view of Mr. Munsey's relations with Mr. Roosevelt, and the financial backing which he furnished to promote

Roosevelt's campaign, it will hardly be questioned that the publication of this editorial was inspired.

Two days later the story that a campaign for Roosevelt was being quietly financed by George W. Perkins of the Steel Trust, and that Ormsby McHarg had been sent into the southern states to "see" the right parties, was printed as coming from Indianapolis, and widely copied in New York, Washington, and other papers. It produced a great sensation. When the newspaper reporters saw Roosevelt at the *Outlook* office to interrogate him on the subject, they experienced considerable difficulty. The session was very brief, and was reported by one of them as follows: "Mr. Roosevelt's jaws snapped shut as he listened, and when they opened it was to say, 'I will not discuss pipe dreams from Indianapolis or anywhere else. There are depths of tomfoolery that I can't notice.' "

But the financing of Roosevelt's campaign by Morgan's friend Perkins was a subject of too great public interest to be disposed of as "tomfoolery." And the watchful newspaper correspondents were soon able to report that private meetings and conferences were being held between Perkins and Roosevelt. The support of Morgan's man, Perkins, recalled to the public mind Roosevelt's great service to the Steel Trust in permitting it to swallow up its principal rival, the Tennessee Coal and Iron Company, and, consequently, the demand for something definite as to Perkins' financial backing of Roosevelt's candidacy became so insistent that it could not be silenced by brushing it aside as a "pipe dream." Some one had to speak, and the speaking part was assigned to Perkins, who issued a "frank statement" announcing that he was supporting Roosevelt because "they looked at public questions in the same way." When taken red-handed the very boldness of an open admission is the best and only recourse. Before many weeks all reserve as to Perkins, Munsey and the Steel Trust was thrown aside, and later men most prominently connected with the Harvester Trust were likewise openly supporting the Roosevelt candidacy. That Wall Street interests generally were in accord was soon well understood among those who noted the kindly references to Roosevelt and the difference in expression whenever his name was mentioned around the Stock Exchange.

While the whole plan in the light of subsequent events became perfectly plain, so cleverly was it all managed, so rapidly were the scenes shifted, so swiftly did the unauthorized announcements and the qualified denials follow one upon the other, that doubt and confusion prevailed everywhere, outside of the little circle of which Roosevelt was the centre. One day it would seem certain that my candidacy had already been betrayed by the friends of Roosevelt who were in my own organization; the next day I would be assured that he would announce his refusal to be a candidate; that there would be no division in the Progressive ranks and that his supporters would be my supporters. But events were driving ahead rapidly. With each day the double play became more difficult. . . .

— Document No. 22 —

THE GOLD BRICK TWINS, 1916 [22]

Typical of Socialist propaganda is the message in this pamphlet issued by the Socialist Party during the 1916 presidential election campaign. Writing in short, precise, and simple language, the author characterizes the Republican and Democratic Parties as the "Gold Brick Twins" and accuses these Parties of working for the interest and benefit of the capitalist class and not for the working class. The Socialists, he insists, are only for those who perform "useful" mental and manual labor.

✓   ✓   ✓

Did you ever buy a gold brick?

Now, don't get indignant. Maybe you have bought gold

[22] John M. Work, *The Gold Brick Twins* (a leaflet issued by the National office of the Socialist Party (Chicago), (1916), 4 pp.)

bricks a good many times without knowing it. If so, it will be well to get your eyes open so you will know a gold brick when you see it.

In case you have at any time in the past voted against your own best interest, this means that you fell for a political confidence game. If you vote against your own best interest this year, it will be proof positive that you are still in the harmless nut stage of development.

No, not so harmless after all, for a few million nuts voting against their own best interest can and do thereby keep the people surrounded by many social evils.

Two of the political parties—the Republican and Democratic Parties—are each trying to put over a gold brick on the people.

Let's take a look at them and size them up.

The Republican platform stands for exaggerated nationalism. The baleful jingo spirit pervades it thruout.

Such scanty labor planks as it contains, on child labor and workmen's compensation, were scared out of the party by the rising Socialist vote. The credit for these planks is therefore due to the Socialist Party, not to the Republican Party.

The suffrage plank, such as it is, was scared out of it by the suffrage organization and the rising Socialist vote. The fact that the women now have the ballot in a number of states was an important factor. When suffrage was unpopular, the Republican Party couldn't see it at all. The plank, however, is a compromise, for it leaves the matter to the states, and sidesteps the question of granting suffrage by amendment of the federal constitution.

But these labor and suffrage planks are, to the Republican Party, minor matters thrown in for the purpose of catching votes. They will do just as little as possible in the way of living up to them, as their record abundantly shows.

The great bulk of the platform is given up to that which the party really stands for—the interests of the capitalist class. Of course they do not say this in so many words. Perish the thought! They are too smooth for that. But it is all there just the same. A strong foreign policy. Horror and indignation concerning the Mexican situation. Hang on to the Philippines. Special privileges to the merchant marine. Encouragement for big business. Protective tariff. A big army and a big navy.

The shameless greed of capitalism smirches the whole platform.

The Democratic platform does not differ from the Republican platform fundamentally at all. Of course, the Democratic convention was held a week later than the Republican, and this gave the Democrats a chance to see what the Republicans had done. Naturally they decided to go the Republicans one better in bidding for the labor vote. Like the Republican Party, the Democratic Party stands for the interests of the capitalist class, and it will do just as little for the working class as it can and get by. The labor planks were frightened out of the Democratic Party by the rising Socialist vote. Therefore the Socialist Party, not the Democratic Party, is entitled to the credit for them.

They also straddle the suffrage question, leaving it to the states. Like the Republicans, they dodged this issue altogether until it became popular.

These scanty labor and suffrage planks are minor matters to the Democratic Party. Their purpose is merely to catch votes.

The great body of the platform is devoted to boasting about the alleged achievements of the Democratic administration, and boosting for nationalism, so-called preparedness, and foreign markets.

The platform says that the life, health and strength of the men, women and children of the nation are its greatest asset.

This is true.

If the platform stood for principles which would give the utmost life, health and strength to the men, women and children of the nation, it would be all right.

But it does not.

On the contrary, after boasting about the achievements of the administration—of which all the good ones were frightened out of it by the rising Socialist vote—they proceed to say that they must now remove, as far as possible, every remaining element of unrest and uncertainty from the path of the business of America and secure for them a continued period of quiet, assured, and confident prosperity.

Do you get that?

If the Democratic Party had ever been anything else than a political representative of capitalism, one could say that this plank is a complete surrender to the capitalist class. But how can a party surrender to those who already own and control it?

This plank merely shows distinctly who does own and control the party. It shows that the party is body and soul the property of the capitalist class. It stands for the continuation of capitalism, with its long and hideous train of woes.

In order to abolish evils, it is entirely necessary to cause unrest and uncertainty among the big business men who profit by the continuance of these evils.

But the Democratic Party says we must not disturb their serenity.

In other words, it stands for the continuation of the great existing social evils.

The Republican and Democratic platforms are more remarkable for what they do not say than for what they do say.

The Republicans and Democrats are fully aware of the fact that hundreds of Americans die of starvation each year. They know that millions of Americans are underfed all the time. They know that hundreds of thousands of Americans are compelled to accept degrading charity. They know that every little while millions of Americans tramp the streets in a vain attempt to find an opportunity to earn a living. They know that thousands of Americans are killed, and hundreds of thousands injured, by preventable accidents. They know that thousands of Americans are driven to suicide. They know that thousands of Americans are driven to insanity. They know that hundreds of thousands of Americans are driven to crime. They know that hundreds of thousands of American women and girls are driven to prostitution. They know that the masses of the American people are in poverty. They know that the masses of the people are compelled to starve themselves mentally, morally, and spiritually in order to keep from starving physically. They know that the private ownership of the industries enables a comparatively few capitalists to get for themselves the bulk of the earnings of the rest of the people.

Do the Republicans and Democratic Parties propose to abolish these evils?

Not on your life.

Why?

Because it is against the interest of the capitalist class to do so—and these parties represent the interest of the capitalist class.

There is no way to abolish these evils except by means of Socialism—and that would abolish the capitalist graft. Therefore the Republican and Democratic Parties are against it.

Furthermore, they seize every pretext to get the people interested in something else, for fear they will flock to the Socialist Party and do away with the capitalist graft. They are willing to make a big noise about fake preparedness, which both of them are in favor of, or any other old humbug, just so they can keep the wool pulled over the eyes of the voters and keep them from voting for their own interests.

For, if the masses of the people vote for their own interests, they will vote the Socialist ticket.

Please get that thoroughly soaked into your head.

If the masses of the people vote for their own interests, they will vote the Socialist ticket.

The private ownership of the exploiting industries gives the capitalists the whip hand over the rest of the people. It enables the capitalists to deliberately appropriate to their own use most of the earnings of the rest of the people—thru profits, dividends, interest, and rent. This keeps the masses of the people impoverished, and results in all the wretched and unnecessary evils which I enumerated above.

The Socialist Party stands for the collective ownership and control of the exploiting industries.

They will then be run for the benefit of all the people, instead of being run for the benefit of a few, as they are now.

Socialism will also guarantee to every willing worker, male and female, an opportunity to earn a living, and to receive his or her full earnings.

This will cause the above mentioned evils to disappear like mist before the morning sun.

The Socialist Party is the party of the working masses.

It stands for the genuine interests of those who do the necessary and useful mental and manual work. It stands for their ultimate interests and also for their immediate interests. Our platform states this very plainly. Read it. You will find that it stands for the collective ownership and control of the exploiting industries. You will also find that it stands for a long list of minor measures, all of which are in the interest of the useful masses of the people. Among them is equal suffrage. We stand for an amendment to the national constitution extending suffrage to women. Our platform has carried an equal suffrage plank ever since the party was organized. We did not wait until it became popular before espousing it. We helped to work it up to the point where it achieved popularity.

Socialism is not hard to understand. Just consider a moment. It is easy to see, is it not, that the benefit of an industry goes to those who own and control it? Practically all the industries are now owned and controlled by capitalists. Therefore the capitalists get the benefit. Socialism will make these industries collectively owned and controlled. Owned by the public. Owned by all the people. Therefore, all the people will get the benefit. The billions of dollars which now go to the useless capitalists will then go to the useful masses.

That is clear, isn't it?

Then vote for it.

Vote the Socialist ticket.

The Republican and Democratic Parties are each trying to put over a gold brick on you.

Are you going to fall for it? . . .

— Document No. 23 —

THE COMMITTEE OF FORTY-EIGHT CALLS FOR A NATIONAL CONVENTION, JULY 10-13, 1920 [23]

The Committee of Forty-eight consisted of a hard core of 1912 Progressives who felt Theodore Roosevelt had betrayed their cause. These Progressives ran several independent state tickets in 1918, and in 1920 determined to take the lead in creating a national Progressive Party. In accordance with this aim, they issued a call for a national convention in Chicago, hoping to cooperate with the Chicago Farmer-Labor convention meeting at the same time. However, discovering the labor representatives did not wish to nominate Robert La Follette and establish a third party, the Committee withdrew. They later took part in the formation of the Conference for Progressive Political Action.

✓   ✓   ✓

To Americans Ready for a New Party

You are invited to attend the National Convention of the Committee of Forty-eight at Chicago, July 10, 12th and 13th, to form a new political party.

It will be a national party representing the needs and hopes of average American men and women. It will conduct an aggressive campaign against both the reactionary old parties and in support of a constructive program of economic, social and political progress. Such a party must be put in the field in the coming election.

For we are witnessing a silent and ominous revolution in our national life. We have seen the tillers of our soil

[23] *La Follette's Magazine*, XII (June, 1920), p. 96.

so discouraged by tenancy, speculation, and the increasing exactions of a swarm of middlemen that hundreds of thousands of them are leaving the farms or curtailing production to a degree that menaces our nation's supply of food.

Prices are mounting while millions of pounds of food are held in storage or cast into the sea in order that still higher prices may be exacted.

We have seen our railroads wrecked by mismanagement and irresponsible financiers and then, after the government had stepped in to repair their injuries and decay, returned to the private management that had despoiled and ruined them, and on terms which arbitrarily guaranteed fixed dividends on watered stocks and bonds, making inevitable a still higher tax on consumption.

We are witnessing the effort to fix a legal status for labor, denying it the right to strike for higher wages, at the same time that profits are legally guaranteed to capital.

This is the underlying cause of the strikes that have increased until all industry is a battlefield of hatred and destruction, and the country is literally going to pieces with factional strife. This system has turned the "New Freedom" into an "Old Slavery" that has changed nothing but its color and its name.

Our moneylenders are seeking to drag us into countless international imbroglios of concessions and investment, the effect of which will be to bind us by secret diplomacy to hazardous agreements entirely alien to our national traditions and desires. This system has so corrupted large sections of our press that the ability to read is fast becoming an impediment to the acquisition of truth. And to crown all, it has desecrated the flag by using it to cover a multitude of sins; and in the name of patriotism has attempted to fasten upon us a degrading economic and political slavery.

Autocracy is a thing abhorrent to us, to any man who has known even the memories of American freedom. We fought it overseas and helped to whip it. We will not yield to it here on our own soil and in our own homes.

Who will lead us in reorganizing and reasserting the American will to independence? It has become clearer with every sun that the old parties cannot do it; that they are but rival lackeys to great monopolies; that they are bankrupt of democratic purposes and have made their peace with a treasonable reaction. No matter which of these two parties wins, the people lose; no matter which of them captures office, it will be to do the bidding of the interests that filled its campaign coffers and paid for its publicity.

The time has come for lovers of the real America to organize themselves anew, to inaugurate another such period of resolute construction as four generations ago raised Jefferson and the once American Democratic party to power, and two generations since raised to power Lincoln and the once American Republican party. Once again constitutional liberties and representative government are threatened and the call goes out for a new political party to restore to America constitutional rights through which the government shall be made responsible to the will of the people.

— Document No. 24 —

ROBERT M. LA FOLLETTE VIEWS THE DEFEAT OF THE PROGRESSIVE PARTY, NOVEMBER, 1924 [24]

Although in 1924 Robert La Follette polled more votes than any other third-party presidential candidate had ever received, he still finished third behind Calvin Coolidge and John W. Davis, the Republican and Democratic nominees. In an article published seven months before he died, La Follette examined the causes of his defeat and sought to rally Progressive forces for the next campaign. How-

[24] Robert M. La Follette, "Forward Progressives for the Campaign of 1926," *La Follette's Magazine*, XVI (November, 1924), p. 165.

*ever, when La Follette died the 1924 Progressive move-
ment died with him.*

✔ ✔ ✔

The American people have returned to power the Republican party with its record of corruption and sub-
servience to the dictates of special Privilege. The sordid
bribery and crookedness of Cabinet officers, the looting of
the Navy's oil reserves through the connivance of officers
of the Navy, the administrative crime of the Federal Reserve Board by which hundreds of thousands of farmers
were deflated and ruined, the attempt to shift the burden
of taxation from the rich to the poor under the Mellon
Tax Plan, the tribute exacted from the people through
the Fordney-McCumber tariff, and the unjustifiable
freight rates under the Esch-Cummins law, were all
prominent issues upon which the Coolidge administration
was arraigned in the campaign which closed on November
fourth.

And yet I am wholly unable to believe that the election
of Mr. Coolidge can be accepted as an endorsement of
the Harding-Coolidge record by the American people. I
have too much faith in the integrity of the plain people of
our country. I believe that the Republican landslide resulted wholly from other causes.

From the first the Progressives carried the fight to the
Republican ticket in the campaign. They proved the
domination of both the Democratic and Republican parties
by the Private Monopoly System. The record of the
Coolidge administration and the frank reactionary platform of the Republican party; the meaningless straddle of
the Democratic platform and the nomination of the private
attorney of J. Pierpont Morgan brought a rising tide of
support to the Independent ticket. During August and
September the reports brought to the managers of the
Republican and Democratic parties showed an amazing
swing to the Progressives which unless checked indicated
the defeat of the old parties.

The Private Monopoly System saw its strangle-hold
upon the government about to be broken. It sounded the
alarm. The industrial, financial, and commercial strength
of the nation was mobilized for action. The money poured
in to the Republican slush fund. The economic thumb-

screws were twisted down upon the farmer, the wage-earner and the independent business man. "Elect Coolidge or Starve" was the slogan. The control of the Private Monopoly System over the economic life of the nation was demonstrated with a vengeance. The fear of hunger and ruin was made to stalk in the homes of the poor, constituting more than seventy per cent of all our people. Notices were posted in the shops that only the foremen need report for work on the Wednesday after election unless Coolidge was elected. The farmers were quietly informed by their bankers that there would be no extension of mortgages unless Coolidge was elected. The merchants whispered to the housewives that prices would advance and that no credit could be had unless Coolidge was elected. Business men were given fat orders subject to cancellation if Coolidge was not elected. The private monopoly system had demonstrated its ability to create a financial panic as far back as 1907. It now demonstrated its ability to create a political panic, the like of which had not been witnessed before in this country.

Under the lash of these masters of America the wonder is not that so many millions were intimidated and voted for Coolidge, but that so many millions stood by their convictions and voted the Independent ticket.

The Progressives will not be dismayed in the face of a defeat which demonstrates that the supreme issue before the American people is to break this combined power of the Private Monopoly System over government and to restore it to the people.

The priceless heritage of our free institutions is not to be yielded up because one battle with the enemy of progressive democracy has been lost. Our ancestors did not surrender in the face of the hardship and suffering of seven long and discouraging years. The hosts of freedom did not despair in the dark hours of the sixties, when human liberty and the union were at stake.

The Progressives will close ranks for the next battle. We are enlisted for life in the struggle to bring government back to the people. We will not quit and we will not compromise. Five million strong, we are determined to break the power of the Private Monopoly System. Without money and with little organization we have shaken the mighty in their seats. We have two years in which to rally and consolidate our forces, perfect every detail of organization, and be fully prepared to face and over-throw the enemy of free government.

Our task is great, but our cause is greater.

Forward Progressives, for the campaign of 1926!

— Document No. 25 —

WORKERS' PARTY PLATFORM, 1924 [25]

In the national elections from 1924 to 1948, the rhetoric and demands of Communist Party platforms remained un-changed. Calling for the abolition of capitalism and the end of the dictatorship of big business, the Communists consistently demanded that the American government be led by the "workers"—industrial and agricultural. In 1924, during their first national campaign, the Com-munists organized the Workers Party as their political action arm. The following selection is a portion of their platform for that year.

✓   ✓   ✓

The workers and exploited farmers of the United States face the question of how to organize and use their polit-ical power in the coming election. Before deciding this question every industrial worker, agricultural worker, and exploited farmer should give fundamental consideration to the situation which exists in this country.

In the Grip of the Exploiters

The United States is the wealthiest country in the world. We have natural resources which supply us with raw ma-terials and a great industrial organization which can turn these raw materials into the finished products which satisfy human needs. With the raw materials available and the tremendous machinery of production we have the means of giving a high standard of life—good food, good cloth-

[25] Chicago *Daily Worker*, August 6, 1924.

ing, good homes, the opportunity for education and recreation—to every person in this country. This high standard of life is denied the workers and exploited farmers of the United States. Millions of these producers of wealth are able to secure for their labor only the means for a bare existence. Millions of workers must work long hours, under bad working conditions, for low wages. Millions are periodically unemployed, as at present, with all the consequent misery and suffering for themselves and their families. In order to keep these conditions from growing worse, millions of industrial workers are periodically compelled to go on strike to fight back the greedy employers. Millions of farmers have been driven into bankruptcy and from the land because of inability to earn enough for a living.

These conditions prevail in a country in which we have the means of supplying a high standard of life to every person because a relatively small class has fastened its grip upon the raw materials and industries and uses these to enrich itself at the expense of the producers. Through theft, fraud, corruption, bribery and the capitalist system of profit taking, this capitalist class has become the owner of the land, raw material and machinery of production upon which the workers and farmers are dependent for a livelihood.

The raw materials and industries of the United States are owned by the Garys, Morgans, Rockefellers, Fords, McCormicks, and other great capitalists. The workers and farmers alike pay tribute to these capitalists. They are compelled to accept a low standard of living in order that the capitalists may amass even greater fortunes for themselves.

It is this system of capitalist ownership of industry which gives the wealth produced to the few, that denies the millions of industrial workers, agricultural workers and exploited farmers the enjoyment of that high standard of life which their labor and the wealth they produce make possible in this country.

It is this system of capitalist ownership of industry which is the basis of the class struggle between the workers, fighting for more of what they produce, and the capitalists, ever bent on securing greater and greater profits for themselves.

How the Capitalists Use the Government

The government of the United States is and has been a government of, by, and for the capitalists. It is through the government and use of the governmental power that the capitalists maintain their grip on the industries and their power to rob the industrial workers, agricultural workers, and farmers.

During the war, with the connivance of government officials, the capitalists looted the country of billions of wealth. Since the war the shipping board deals, the war veterans' board corruption, the Teapot Dome exposures, have shown how the capitalists fill their pockets at the expense of the working and farming masses . . .

The government is a dictatorship of the capitalists and their instrument for the oppression and exploitation of the workers. Although the workers are permitted to vote, the capitalists are able, through their control of the means of information and through their economic power, to completely dominate the government, national, state and local.

The Election This Year

It is these conditions which the workers and exploited farmers must consider in using their political power in the election this year.

The capitalist dictatorship has named two candidates, the Republican, strike-breaker Coolidge, and the Morgan-Rockefeller lawyer Davis. Both are agents of the capitalist class. They, and the other candidates of the two old parties, will loyally serve the capitalists if returned to power—as they have done in the past.

La Follette, who is running as an independent, progressive Republican, is equally a supporter of the capitalist system of exploitation. The only difference between La Follette and Coolidge and Davis is that La Follette represents the independent manufacturers, bankers and merchants, who are seeking greater power and profit for themselves and are trying to use the workers and farmers to attain that end.

La Follette is the representative of little business against big business, but not the representative of the workers and exploited farmers in their struggle against the capitalists. La Follette's platform is not a workers' and farmers' platform, but a little business men's platform with some bait thrown in for sections of the skilled workers.

Against these three candidates of the capitalist system of exploitation, big and little, the Workers' (Communist) Party presents working class candidates—Foster and Gitlow—and a working class platform.

The Workers Must Rule

There is only one way in which the exploitation of the workers and farmers of this country can be ended. That is through the workers organizing their mass power, ending the capitalist dictatorship and establishing the Workers' and Farmers' Government. . . .

— Document No. 26 —

PROGRESSIVE PARTY PLATFORM, 1948[26]

Communists and their close allies wrote most of the Progressive Party platform of 1948. These individuals were not a majority of the platform committee, but enough non-Communists agreed with some parts of the party line to allow the Communists to dominate the proceedings. Lee Pressman, who earlier in 1948 had been eased from his position in the CIO national office because of his Communist sympathies, directed the writing of the first or "New York" draft of the platform. University of Chicago's Rexford G. Tugwell, chairman of the platform committee, quietly withdrew from party activity before the election as he came to realize that the Progressive movement was Communist-controlled.

1   1   1

[26] Kirk H. Porter and Donald B. Johnson, compilers, *National Party Platforms, 1840-1956* (Urbana, Ill., 1956) pp. 436-437.

Preamble

Three years after the end of the second world war, the drums are beating for a third. Civil liberties are being destroyed. Millions cry out for relief from unbearably high prices. The American way of life is in danger.

The root cause of this crisis is Big Business control of our economy and government.

With toil and enterprise the American people have created from their rich resources the world's greatest productive machine. This machine no longer belongs to the people. Its ownership is concentrated in the hands of a few and its product used for their enrichment.

Never before have so few owned so much at the expense of so many.

Ten years ago Franklin Delano Roosevelt warned: "The liberty of a democracy is not safe if the people tolerate the growth of private power to a point where it becomes stronger than their democratic state. That, in its essence, is fascism."

Today that private power has constituted itself an invisible government which pulls the strings of its puppet Republican and Democratic parties. Two sets of candidates compete for votes under the outworn emblems of the old parties. But both represent a single program—a program of monopoly profits through war preparations, lower living standards, and suppression of dissent.

For generations the common man of America has resisted this concentration of economic and political power in the hands of a few. The greatest of America's political leaders have led the people into battle against the money power, the railroads, the trusts, the economic royalists.

We of the Progressive Party are the present-day descendants of these people's movements and fighting leaders. We are the political heirs of Jefferson, Jackson and Lincoln—of Frederick Douglass, Altgeld, and Debs—of "Fighting Bob" La Follette, George Norris, and Franklin Roosevelt.

Throughout our history new parties have arisen when the old parties have betrayed the people. As Jefferson headed a new party to defeat the reactionaries of his day, and as Lincoln led a new party to victory over the slave-owners, so today the people, inspired and led by Henry

Wallace, have created a new party to secure peace, freedom, and abundance. . . .

Betrayal by the Old Parties

The American people want peace. But the old parties, obedient to the dictates of monopoly and the military, prepare for war in the name of peace.

They refuse to negotiate a settlement of differences with the Soviet Union.

They reject the United Nations as an instrument for promoting world peace and reconstruction.

They use the Marshall Plan to rebuild Nazi Germany as a war base and to subjugate the economies of other European countries to American Big Business.

They finance and arm corrupt, fascist governments in China, Greece, Turkey, and elsewhere, through the Truman Doctrine, wasting billions in American resources and squandering America's heritage as the enemy of despotism.

They encircle the globe with military bases which other peoples cannot but view as threats to their freedom and security.

They protect the war-making industrial and financial barons of Nazi Germany and imperial Japan, and restore them to power.

They stockpile atomic bombs.

They pass legislation to admit displaced persons, discriminating against Catholics, Jews, and other victims of Hitler.

They impose a peacetime draft and move toward Universal Military Training.

They fill policy-making positions in government with generals and Wall Street bankers.

Peace cannot be won—but profits can—by spending ever-increasing billions of the people's money in war preparations.

Yet these are the policies of the two old parties—policies profaning the name of peace.

The American people cherish freedom.

But the old parties, acting for the forces of special privilege, conspire to destroy traditional American freedoms.

They deny the Negro people the rights of citizenship. They impose a universal policy of Jim Crow and enforce it with every weapon of terror. They refuse to outlaw its most bestial expression—the crime of lynching.

They refuse to abolish the poll tax, and year after year they deny the right to vote to Negroes and millions of white people in the South.

They aim to reduce nationality groups to a position of social, economic, and political inferiority.

They connive to bar the Progressive Party from the ballot.

They move to outlaw the Communist Party as a decisive step in their assault on the democratic rights of labor, of national, racial, and political minorities, and of all those who oppose their drive to war. In this they repeat the history of Nazi Germany, Fascist Italy, and Franco Spain.

They support the House Committee on Un-American Activities in its vilification and persecution of citizens in total disregard of the Bill of Rights.

They build the Federal Bureau of Investigation into a political police with secret dossiers on millions of Americans.

They seek to regiment the thinking of the American people and to suppress political dissent.

They strive to enact such measures as the Mundt-Nixon Bill which are as destructive of democracy as were the Alien and Sedition Laws against which Jefferson fought.

They concoct a spurious "loyalty" program to create an atmosphere of fear and hysteria in government and industry.

They shackle American labor with the Taft-Hartley Act at the express command of Big Business, while encouraging exorbitant profits through uncontrolled inflation.

They restore the labor injunction as a weapon for breaking strikes and smashing Unions.

This is the record of the two old parties—a record profaning the American ideal of freedom.

The American people want abundance.

But the old parties refuse to enact effective price and rent controls, making the people victims of a disastrous inflation which dissipates the savings of millions of families and depresses their living standards.

They ignore the housing problem, although more than half the nation's families including millions of veterans, are homeless or living in rural and urban slums.

They refuse social security protection to millions and allow only meagre benefits to the rest.

They block national health legislation even though millions of men, women, and children are without adequate medical care.

They foster the concentration of private economic power.

They replace progressive government officials, the supporters of Franklin Roosevelt, with spokesmen of Big Business.

They pass tax legislation for the greedy, giving only insignificant reductions to the needy.

These are the acts of the old parties—acts profaning the American dream of abundance.

No glittering party platforms or election promises of the Democratic and Republican parties can hide their betrayal of the needs of the American people.

Nor can they act otherwise. For both parties, as the record of the 80th Congress makes clear, are the champions of Big Business.

The Republican platform admits it.

The Democratic platform attempts to conceal it.

But the very composition of the Democratic leadership exposes the demogogy of its platform. It is a party of machine politicians and Southern Bourbons who veto in Congress the liberal planks "won" in convention.

Such platforms, conceived in hypocrisy and lack of principle, deserve nothing but contempt.

Principles of the Progressive Party

The Progressive Party is born in the deep conviction that the national wealth and natural resources of our country belong to the people who inhabit it and must be employed in their behalf; that freedom and opportunity must be secured equally to all; that the brotherhood of man can be achieved and scourge of war ended.

The Progressive Party holds that basic to the organization of world peace is a return to the purposes of Franklin Roosevelt to seek areas of international agreement rather than disagreement. It was his conviction that within the framework of the United Nations different social and economic systems can and must live together. If peace is to be achieved capitalist United States and communist Russia must establish good relations and work together.

The Progressive Party holds that it is the first duty of a just government to secure for all the people, regardless of race, creed, color, sex, national background, political belief, or station in life, the inalienable rights proclaimed in the Declaration of Independence and guaranteed by the Bill of Rights. The government must actively protect these rights against the encroachments of public and private agencies.

The Progressive Party holds that a just government must use its powers to promote an abundant life for its people. This is the basic idea of Franklin Roosevelt's Economic Bill of Rights. Heretofore every attempt to give effect to this principle has failed because Big Business dominates the key sectors of the economy. Antitrust laws and government regulation cannot break this domination. Therefore the people, through their democratically elected representatives, must take control of the main levers of the economic system. Public ownership of these levers will enable the people to plan the use of their productive resources so as to develop the limitless potential of modern technology and to create a true American-Commonwealth free from poverty and insecurity.

The Progressive Party believes that only through peaceful understanding can the world make progress toward reconstruction and higher standards of living; that peace is the essential condition for safe-guarding and extending our traditional freedoms; that only by preserving liberty and by planning an abundant life for all can we eliminate the sources of world conflict. Peace, freedom, and abundance—the goals of the Progressive Party—are indivisible.

Only the Progressive Party can destroy the power of private monopoly and restore the government to the American people. For ours is a party uncorrupted by privilege, committed to no special interests, free from machine control, and open to all Americans of all races, colors, and creeds.

The Progressive Party is a party of action. We seek through the democratic process and through day-by-day activity to lead the American people toward the fulfillment of these principles. . . .

BIBLIOGRAPHY

GENERAL STUDIES

Binkley, Wilfred E., *American Political Parties, Their Natural History* (New York, 1944).

Haynes, Frederick E., *Social Politics in the United States* (Boston, 1924).

————, *Third Party Movements Since the Civil War, with Special Reference to Iowa: a Study in Social Politics* (Iowa City, 1916).

Hesseltine, William B., *Rise and Fall of Third Parties, From Anti-Masonry to Wallace* (Washington, 1948).

Hofstadter, Richard, *Age of Reform* (New York, 1955).

McKee, Thomas H., *National Conventions and Platforms of all Political Parties, 1789-1900* (Baltimore, 1900).

Nash, Howard P. Jr., *Third Parties in American Politics* (Washington, 1959).

Porter, Kirk H., and Donald B. Johnson, compilers, *National Party Platforms, 1840-1956* (Urbana, Ill., 1956).

Robinson, E. E., *The Evolution of American Political Parties* (New York, 1924).

Stedman, Murry S., and Susan Stedman, *Discontent at the Polls: A Study of Farmer and Labor Parties, 1827-1948,* (New York, 1950).

ANTIMASONIC PARTY

Current, Richard N., *Old Thad Stevens* (Madison, Wis., 1948).

Hammond, Jabez, *A History of the Political Parties in the State of New York* (3 vols. Syracuse, N. Y., 1852).

McCarthy, Charles, *The Anti-Masonic Party: a Study of Political Anti-Masonry in the United States, 1827-1840*, American Historical Association *Annual Report* (1902), I:367-574.

Van Deusen, Glyndon C., *Thurlow Weed, Wizard of the Lobby* (Boston, 1947).

ANTIRENT PARTY

Ellis, David Maldwyn, *Landlords and Farmers in the Hudson-Mohawk Region, 1790-1850* (Ithaca, N. Y., 1946).

COMMUNIST PARTY

Howe, Irving, and Lewis Coser with the assistance of Julius Jacobson, *The American Communist Party: a Critical History, 1919-1957* (Boston, 1957).

Shannon, David A., *The Decline of American Communism: a History of the Communist Party of the United States since 1945* (New York, 1959).

FREE SOIL AND LIBERTY PARTIES

Bretz, Julian P., "Economic Background of the Liberty Party," *American Historical Review*, XXXIV (January 1929), 250-265.

Donovan, Herbert D. A., *The Barnburners* (New York, 1925).

Filler, Louis, *The Crusade Against Slavery, 1830-1860* (New York, 1960).

Fladeland, Betty, *James Gillespie Birney: Slaveholder to Abolitionist* (Ithaca, N. Y., 1955).

Smith, Theodore C., *Liberty and Free Soil Parties in the Northwest* (New York, 1897).

GREENBACK AND LABOR PARTIES

Buck, Solon J., *The Agrarian Crusade* (New Haven, 1920).

Commons, John R., *et al*, *History of Labour in the United States* (4 vols. New York, 1918-1935), II.

Fine, Nathan, *Labor and Farmer Parties in the United States, 1828-1928* (New York, 1929).

Haynes, Frederick E., *James Baird Weaver* (Iowa City, 1919).

KNOW-NOTHING AND NATIVIST PARTIES

Billington, Ray Allen, *The Protestant Crusade, 1800-1860: a Study in the Origins of American Nativism* (New York, 1938).

Hesseltine, William B., and Rex G. Fisher, *Trimmers, Trucklers and Temporizers: Notes of Murat Halstead on the 1856 Political Conventions* (Madison, Wis., 1961).

Overdyke, W. Darrell, *The Know Nothing Party in the South* (Baton Rouge, 1950).

Scisco, Louis D., "Political Nativism in New York State," Columbia University *Studies in History, Economics, and Public Law*, XIII, No. 2 (1901).

Schmeckebier, L. F., "History of the Know-Nothing Party in Maryland," Johns Hopkins University *Studies in Historical and Political Science*, XVII (1899).

Shugg, Roger W., *Origins of Class Struggle in Louisiana: a Social History of White Farmers and Laborers during Slavery and after, 1840-1875* (Baton Rouge, 1939).

LABOR PARTIES (see GREENBACK AND LABOR PARTIES).

LIBERTY PARTY (see FREE SOIL AND LIBERTY PARTIES)

LIBERAL REPUBLICANS

Ross, E. D., *The Liberal Republican Movement* (New York, 1919).

LOCO-FOCO PARTY (see WORKINGMEN'S AND LOCO-FOCO PARTIES)

NATIVIST PARTY (see KNOW-NOTHING AND NATIVIST PARTIES)

PROGRESSIVE PARTIES

Bowers, Claude G., *Beveridge and the Progressive Era* (Bostón, 1932).

La Follette, Robert M., *La Follette's Autobiography* (Madison, 1960).

MacKay, Kenneth C., *The Progressive Movement of 1924* (New York, 1947).

Maxwell, Robert S., *La Follette and the Rise of the Progressives in Wisconsin* (Madison, 1956).

Mowry, George E., *Theodore Roosevelt and the Progressive Movement* (Madison, Wis., 1946).

Nye, Russell B., *Midwestern Progressive Politics: a Historical Study of its Origin and Development, 1870-1950* (East Lansing, Mich., 1951).

Pinchot, Amos, *History of the Progressive Party, 1912-1916,* edited with a biographical introduction by Helene Maxwell Hooker (New York, 1958).

Schmidt, Karl M., *Henry A. Wallace: Quixotic Crusader, 1948* (Syracuse, N. Y., 1960).

PROHIBITION PARTY

Byrne, Frank L., *Prophet of Prohibition: Neal Dow and his Crusade* (Madison, Wis., 1961).

Colvin, David L., *Prohibition in the United States: a History of the Prohibition Party and of the Prohibition Movement* (New York, 1926).

POPULIST PARTY

Destler, Chester M., *American Radicalism, 1865-1901: Essays and Documents* (New London, Conn., 1946).

Hicks, John D., *The Populist Revolt: a History of the Farmer's Alliance and People's Party* (Minneapolis, 1931).

Martin, Roscoe C., "The People's Party in Texas: a Study in Third Party Politics," The University of Texas *Bulletin*, No. 3308 (1933).

Miller, Raymond C., "The Background of Populism in Kansas," *Mississippi Valley Historical Review*, XI (March 1925), pp. 469-489.

Sheldon, William DuBose, *Populism in the Old Dominion: Virginia Farm Politics, 1885-1900* (Princeton, 1935).

SOCIALIST PARTY

Quint, Howard H., *The Forging of American Socialism: Origins of the Modern Movement* (Columbia, S. C., 1953).

Shannon, David A., *The Socialist Party of America: a History* (New York, 1956).

Kipnis, Ira, *The American Socialist Movement, 1897-1912* (New York, 1952).

WORKINGMEN'S AND LOCO-FOCO PARTIES

Byrdsall, Fitzwilliam, *History of the Loco Foco or Equal Rights Party* (New York, 1842).

Commons, John R., *et al, History of Labour in the United States* (4 vols. New York, 1918-1935), I.

Hugins, Walter E., *Jacksonian Democracy and the Working Class: a Study of the New York Workingmen's Movement, 1824-1837* (Stanford, Calif., 1960).

Zorn, Roman J., "The Workingmen's Parties of 1828-1831," Arkansas Academy of Science *Proceedings*, IV (1951), 173-181.

INDEX

VAN NOSTRAND ANVIL BOOKS already published

1 *MAKING OF MODERN FRENCH MIND*—H. Kohn
2 *THE AMERICAN REVOLUTION*—R. B. Morris
3 *THE LATE VICTORIANS*—H. Ausubel
4 *WORLD IN THE 20th CENTURY*—L. L. Snyder
5 *50 DOCUMENTS OF THE 20th CENTURY*—
   L. L. Snyder
6 *THE AGE OF REASON*—L. L. Snyder
7 *MARX AND THE MARXISTS*—S. Hook
8 *NATIONALISM*—H. Kohn
9 *MODERN JAPAN*—A. Tiedemann
10 *50 DOCUMENTS OF THE 19th CENTURY*—
   L. L. Snyder
11 *CONSERVATISM*—P. Viereck
12 *THE PAPACY*—J. A. Corbett
13 *AGE OF THE REFORMATION*—R. H. Bainton
14 *DOCUMENTS IN AMERICAN HISTORY*—
   R. B. Morris
15 *CONTEMPORARY AFRICA*—T. W. Wallbank
16 *THE RUSSIAN REVOLUTIONS OF 1917*—J. S. Curtiss
17 *THE GREEK MIND*—W. R. Agard
18 *BRITISH CONSTITUTIONAL HISTORY SINCE 1832*
   —R. L. Schuyler and C. C. Weston
19 *THE NEGRO IN THE U.S.*—R. W. Logan
20 *AMERICAN CAPITALISM*—L. M. Hacker
21 *LIBERALISM*—J. S. Schapiro
22 *ERA OF THE FRENCH REVOLUTION, 1789-1799*—
   L. Gershoy
23 *HISTORY OF MODERN GERMANY*—L. L. Snyder
24 *HISTORY OF MODERN RUSSIA*—H. Kohn
25 *NORTH ATLANTIC CIVILIZATION*—M. Kraus
26 *NATO*—M. Salvadori
27 *DOCUMENTS IN U.S. FOREIGN POLICY*—
   T. P. Brockway
28 *AMERICAN FARMERS' MOVEMENTS*—
   F. A. Shannon
29 *HISTORIC DECISIONS OF SUPREME COURT*—
   C. B. Swisher
30 *MEDIEVAL TOWN*—J. H. Mundy and P. Riesenberg
31 *REVOLUTION AND REACTION 1848-1852*—
   G. Bruun
32 *SOUTHEAST ASIA AND WORLD TODAY*—
   C. A. Buss
33 *HISTORIC DOCUMENTS OF W. W. I*—L. L. Snyder
34 *HISTORIC DOCUMENTS OF W. W. II*—
   W. C. Langsam
35 *ROMAN MIND AT WORK*—P. MacKendrick